Can You RELATE?

How to Handle Parents, Friends, Boys, and More

Vicki Courtney

B&H
PUBLISHING GROUP
Nashville, Tennessee

This book is dedicated to my sweet tween-age niece, Tatum. I am so grateful that God picked me to be your aunt!

Published in association with the literary agency D.C. Jacobson & Associates, LLC, an Author Management Company, www.dcjacobson.com, and Alive Communications, Inc., an Author Management Company, www.alivecommunications.com.

978-1-4336-8785-3

Published by B&H Publishing Group
Nashville, Tennessee

Dewey Decimal Classification: 302
INTERPERSONAL RELATIONS / GIRLS /TEENAGERS

Printed in October 2015 in LongGang District, Shenzhen, China

1 2 3 4 5 6   20 19 18 17 16

Introduction

In an old box of keepsakes from my childhood, I recently found an old calendar from sixth grade. I wasn't much into keeping a journal or a diary, but I filled in each daily box in the month of January with highlights of my day. After that, I must have given up because the calendar pages for February through December were completely blank. Except of course in May, when I wrote in bold marker and all caps: *LAST DAY OF SCHOOL!!* Who could leave out that important detail?!

It was fun to look at the January calendar page and get a snapshot of my now forgotten sixth-grade self. Here is a taste of what I found on the calendar page:

January 6: I went ice-skating with Belinda. I skated backward for about 30 seconds before I fell!

January 10: Dorwin asked me to go steady again. I said "no."

(Note: "Going steady" is what we called "going out." But you don't go anywhere, of course!)

January 12: David asked me out. I said "yes," but he broke up after 3 hours.

January 14: My brother accidentally shot me in the fingernail with his BB gun, and it turned purple. He is so grounded.

January 18: I told my friends I would not go with another boy for one month.

January 20: I really, really like Mark R.

January 23: I found out Mark R. likes Missy. :(

January 25: Spent the night at Kara's house, and we did back flips off the back of her parents' bed.

January 28: Mrs. Coop read one of my notes out loud in class. Embarrassing.

I think we can sum up my sixth-grade self as a boy-crazy-loves-her-friends-but-wants-her-annoying-brother-to-disappear kind of girl. Clearly, relationships were important in my life as a tween girl. Maybe you could even say they were my whole world. Relationships with friends, family, and yikes, even boys. Can you relate?

Can You Relate? is a guide to help you through all the relationships that are important in your life. Whether you read this book on your own or grab a group of girls and use it for a Bible study or book club, I pray it will help you celebrate the blessing of relationships and relate better to your family, friends, the world, and most importantly, God.

Vicki Courtney

P.S. As you read, you'll find several QR codes with questions next to them. Using any QR reader app, scan the codes to connect to some fun videos of girls giving their answers to the questions. Maybe you'll relate to what they have to say!

When you see a QR code like this, scan it!

About the writers

Vicki Courtney is a speaker and best-selling author of numerous books and Bible studies. She began writing about the culture's influence on tween and teen girls in 2003 and has a passion to see girls and women of all ages find their worth in Christ. Vicki is married to Keith, and they live in Austin, Texas. They are parents to three grown children, who are all married and live nearby. Vicki enjoys spending time at the lake, hanging out with her family, and spoiling her grandchildren rotten. More information about Vicki can be found at VickiCourtney.com.

Pam Gibbs (project editor) is a writer, editor, speaker, youth minister, and amateur archer, but her favorite titles are wife and mom. She is a graduate of Southwestern Baptist Theological Seminary and leads teens at her church. When she's not hanging out with her tween daughter and teacher/coach husband, you'll find her curled up with a good mystery book and some dark chocolate.

Susie Davis is the author of *Unafraid: Trusting God in an Unsafe World.* She and her husband, Will, co-founded Austin Christian Fellowship, where they pastor some of the most fabulous people in town. Susie loves McDonald's coffee, pink geraniums, and the yellow finches that flood her backyard every morning. For more info, visit her website at susiedavis.org

Susan Palacio has served professionally in ministry and missions for ten years, including a two-year stint serving in Guatemala. She is passionate about Truth and loves teaching women and girls. Susan and her husband, Carlos, live in Flower Mound, Texas, with their daughter, Emma, and are the owners of a coffee shop (Trio Craft Coffee), which they opened for the purpose of "business as mission."

Whitney Prosperi has a heart for girls and girls' ministry. She is the author of *Life Style: Real Perspectives from Radical Women in the Bible*, a twelve-week Bible study for middle and high school girls, as well as *Girls' Ministry 101*, published by Youth Specialties. She lives in Tyler, Texas, with her husband, Randy, and daughters, Annabelle and Libby.

Contents

FRIENDS

Are YOU an Awesome Friend?

by Susie Davis

Your friends are some of the most important people in your life. You spend tons of time with them. You laugh with them, goof around with them, and share secrets with them. Because friends matter so much, it's important to know how best to get along with them. What better place than the Bible to get some tips on how to be a good friend? Here's a girl's guide to friendship—with verses from the Bible to show you how to be the kind of friend everyone would want!

Be selfless.

Let's be honest—most people think of themselves first. Whether you are in line at school or playing your favorite sport, thinking about yourself comes naturally. But Philippians 2:4 says, "Everyone should look out not only for his own interests, but also for the interests of others." This verse tells us to think about other people too. In fact, Jesus challenged His followers (that's you and me!) to be last instead of first (Matthew 20:26–28).

One of my good friends gave me an idea on how to be selfless with others. It's called the "second cookie" rule. It goes something like this: Pretend you and your friend are at your house, and your mom has just made a batch of homemade cookies. She hands you the plate. What do you do? Do you grab the biggest cookie and stuff it in your mouth? Not if you want to be selfless. The "second cookie" rule is to let your friends pick first. You take the "second cookie."

This rule works in other areas too. What about choosing to let your friend pick the game or movie? Or maybe let your friend borrow a book you were saving for yourself? A good friend doesn't need to be first, doesn't need to have her way all the time, and doesn't compete for bragging rights.

Be a secret keeper.

Being a secret keeper is a must for friends. Ask one hundred girls about the qualities they want in a friend, and you will hear this answer over and over. Sometimes it seems like girls struggle with this—it's hard for us to keep our mouths shut! Proverbs 11:13 says, "A gossip goes around revealing a secret, but a trustworthy person keeps a confidence." This verse highlights the importance of being trustworthy. That means people can have confidence in you—you are worthy of their trust. In friendships, you should earn others' trust by your ability to keep a secret. When a person shares a secret, she trusts you with a little piece of her heart. If you are revealing secrets, you're a gossip, and "a gossip separates close friends" (Proverbs 16:28). Decide now that you will be a secret keeper.

Keeping secrets has its limits. If you find out that a friend is in real trouble, you can't keep that a secret. For example, if a friend is being abused or bullied, you need to tell an adult. Your parents would be a good place to turn. Sometimes, the best thing you can do for a friend is NOT to keep a secret.

Be a forgiver.

Friends will hurt you. Even your best friends can let you down. (Remember, Jesus had friends who let Him down.) Because disagreements and hurt feelings are just a part of being friends with others, you must choose whether or not to forgive when someone hurts you. Proverbs 17:9 promises: "Whoever conceals an offense promotes love, but whoever gossips about it separates friends." An *offense* is when someone hurts you—lies to you, makes a joke about you, gets a boyfriend and blows you off. When that happens (and it will!), the Bible challenges you to let it go. If you do, that forgiveness will bond (glue together) a friendship. If you don't forgive but instead stay bitter and angry, the Bible predicts that you'll be saying goodbye to that friendship.

Be open and available.

Don't fall into the trap of having only one friend. Having a best friend is great, but that friend cannot be your only friend. One friend can only do so much, and if you lean on your one best friend for everything, you will end up disappointed, and she will end up frustrated. Instead, decide to be a friend to many different people. Get to know lots of kids in your school, church, and neighborhood. You can be friends with many of them. As a bonus, you won't be known as that girl who only stays in one group of friends.

Be friends with the best friend ever.

In John 15:13, Jesus said, "No one has greater love than this, that someone would lay down his life for his friends." Did you know that Jesus died just for you? He literally gave His life so that those who believe in Him could have eternal life (life in heaven after you die) and a relationship with God that begins the moment you trust in Him. You will find no better friend than Jesus Christ. He will never stop loving you. He will never stop caring for you. He will never spread gossip, start rumors, or tell others your secrets. He will never run out of time for you. Never. As friends in your life come and go, Jesus Christ remains the same yesterday, today, and forever. And because of that promise, you can count on His constant, loving friendship throughout your life. So get to know Him well; as you do, you will discover that He is the best friend ever.

Are You a Faithful Friend?

by Susan Palacio

Faithfulness is an important characteristic to have in friendship. If you look up *faithful* in the dictionary, you might find: "true to one's word, promises" or "reliable, trusted, or believed" in the description. Just like God is faithful to us, He expects us to be faithful to others. Finish these stories to find out if you're a faithful friend!

What If #1

You and your best friend _____ (name of BFF) are inseparable.

You do everything together, from _____ (fun outside activity) and

_____ (fun inside activity) to _____ (fun church activity).

One of your favorite things to do is listen to _____ (favorite singer/

band) together and sing along. Sometimes you even act as if you're auditioning for

_____ (TV talent contest), and you each take turns trying out.

You dreamed about going to see _____ (favorite singer/band) one day.

Your mom knew that you loved _____ (favorite singer/band)

and heard that _____ (he/she/they) was/were coming to

_____ (city where you live) for a concert. For your birthday, she

got you a ticket plus an extra one to invite a friend. When you open the gift you scream

_____ (whatever you normally scream when you're excited). Your ex-

citement level is at a _____ (number 1–100). Next comes the hard part—who to invite.

For as long as you can remember, you've always wanted to be friends with _____

(popular girl's name). She is super popular, and everyone wants to hang out with her because

_____ (I don't know—you tell me).

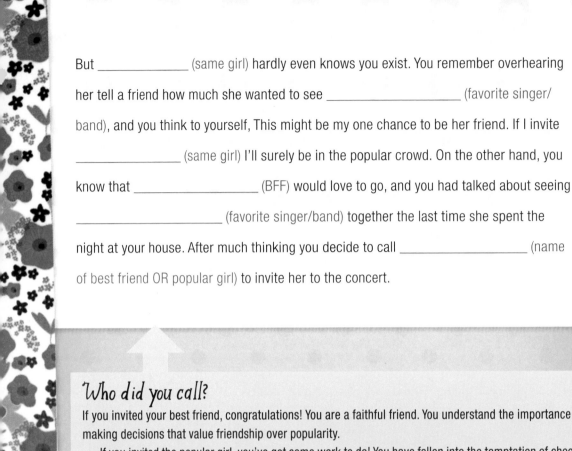

But _____ (same girl) hardly even knows you exist. You remember overhearing her tell a friend how much she wanted to see _____ (favorite singer/band), and you think to yourself, This might be my one chance to be her friend. If I invite _____ (same girl) I'll surely be in the popular crowd. On the other hand, you know that _____ (BFF) would love to go, and you had talked about seeing _____ (favorite singer/band) together the last time she spent the night at your house. After much thinking you decide to call _____ (name of best friend OR popular girl) to invite her to the concert.

Who did you call?

If you invited your best friend, congratulations! You are a faithful friend. You understand the importance of making decisions that value friendship over popularity.

If you invited the popular girl, you've got some work to do! You have fallen into the temptation of choosing popularity over genuine friendship. Put yourself in your BFF's shoes. How would your (pretend) decision make you feel? Don't despair; God can teach us a lot about how to be faithful!

Where did you end up?

If you went to the first friend's house, good job! You were faithful to the first invitation you had for the evening. You realize that it's better to honor your friend by not ditching her invitation just because something better came up.

If you went to the cool girl's house, think about this: Would you really be able to have fun knowing that you blew off your other friend? Sometimes it's easy to find an excuse to make it "okay" to do something we know we shouldn't. You hadn't exactly committed to the friend on your sports team, so if you accepted the other invitation really quickly you could honestly say that you had other plans. In a way, that's kind of like cheating. Deep down, you knew the right thing to do, but you didn't do it. Making poor decisions like this now can set you on a path to give bigger excuses later in life. Start making better choices today!

What If #2

Your friend from _____ (sport you play/have tried) called or texted to invite you

over to her house on _____ (weekend night) night for _____

(favorite food) and a movie. You're _____ (positive expressive adjective)

because you really like her. You tell _____ (friend) you'd love to but have

to check with your _____ (mom or dad) first just to make sure. You shout

with all your might to _____ (mom or dad) downstairs to get permission, when

suddenly you hear a knock on the door. It's _____ (a different girl's name),

who lives in your neighborhood! She's the "cool kid" on the block and is dropping by to tell you

about a party at her house on _____ (same weekend night) night. She's never

invited you to anything! You are sooooo _____ (positive expressive adjective),

and you are just about to accept the invitation when you realize that her party is the same night

that _____ (name of girl on your sports team) invited you over. You decide

to tell both girls that you'll get back to them.

   You'd rather go to _____ (cool kid's name)'s house for the party. You

think to yourself, I could always make up an excuse to get out of _____

(name of girl on your sports team)'s invitation. But _____ (name of girl on

your sports team) asked you first. You think about it for a while and ultimately decide to go to

_____ (either cool kid OR sport girl's name)'s house.

Oh, Snap!

Dealing with Girl Drama

by Pam Gibbs

You walk into the cafeteria from math class, thrilled that your teacher didn't call on you to do a problem on the board. The moment you step through the doorway, you can tell that something is wrong. You look across the room and see it: two friends who normally sit together are sitting in opposite corners of the room. This can't be good. By the end of the day, the stories are flying through the hallways—about what one girl did to the other and how the other girl got back at her. Before long, half the girls in your school (it seems) have picked a side.

What do you do?

Girl drama is a part of life as a tween. Friendships are very important, and sometimes those friendships—close or not-so-close—get messed up. Words are said. Feelings are hurt. Emotions get in the way. And, unfortunately, some girls like to stir things up. It's like they feed on it. They like being the center of the drama.

Although you can't always avoid girl drama, you can take some steps to make sure you don't get in the center of the drama or make it worse. Try out these ideas:

Be nice.

I know it sounds simple, but simply being nice to those around you can create more peace and less stress. Being nice means helping a classmate with an assignment, letting someone else go first in line, letting someone else speak first, listening, smiling. Kind behavior can be contagious.

Ignore rumors, and don't spread them.

Rumors are like trying to play with fire without getting burned. Just don't go there. Ignore what you hear in the hallways. About 99 percent of it is just rumors. And never, ever spread rumors. Not only do you look like a big gossip, but you are also fueling the fire of hatred and hurt. Nothing good comes from paying attention to rumors or passing them along. If you like to share them because you feel important, it's time to check your heart.

Mind your own business.

Don't get involved in a fight between two girls. Even if you are totally convinced one girl is right and the other is wrong, don't choose sides. You cannot judge because you don't really know all the facts. Stay neutral (in the middle— don't choose a side). Don't get involved. Stay out of the way. When you take sides, you risk the chance of becoming the topic of gossip or the target of another girl's anger.

Ignore people who pick on others.

People who pick on others are just looking for attention. The more attention they get, the more they will pick on others. Don't encourage their behavior by laughing. If the situation gets worse, tell an adult quickly.

Keep your secrets to yourself.

Be very careful about who you share them with. You can always talk to your mom and dad or your siblings (no, that's not lame!) or a really, really close friend. You might be tempted to share your secrets during a sleepover or while a bunch of you are hanging out in a group. Don't. In a group of friends, you may think you are close to all of them, but you may find out the hard way that you aren't when one of those girls shares your secret with someone else and so on and so on. Next thing you know, your secret becomes the hottest news in school.

Be okay with girls having different opinions.

One friend might think the latest boy band is awesome even though you think they are totally lame and immature. That doesn't mean you need to explain that fact to her at lunch with ten girls around. That's just asking for girl drama. You can share your opinion, but be polite about it. Avoid saying, "That group is stupid." Just say, "You know, I like _____ instead. Have you ever heard of them?" See the difference? *How* you say something is just as important as what you say.

Check your emotions.

If you're in a bad mood, you might not want to go hang with the girls at the park. You might spread that mood to the other girls and get into a fight with them. Before you make a rude comment or a sarcastic remark, check your emotions. Why are you so cranky? Sad? Frustrated? Angry? Be careful not to let your emotions get the best of you. That's *exactly* how a lot of girl drama starts.

Have different groups of friends.

Many girls have one group of friends at school, another group of friends at church, and other friends who are in their neighborhood or an after-school activity. When the drama rises in one place, they can back away and go hang with another group of friends. Be careful about only having one group of friends. If that group ever has trouble, you're likely to be smack in the middle of it with nowhere to turn. And that's a bad place to be.

I'm-so-over-it drama is not worth it. Keep away from drama and keep the friendships instead.

When a Friend Is Boy Crazy

by Vicki Courtney

Boys. One minute they're fun to be around, and the next they're burping the alphabet, ignoring you, and acting sooooo immature.

At your age, it's normal to notice guys. It's also normal not to care about them much at all—at least not in the "boyfriend" sort of way. Maybe you're one of the girls who doesn't care much about liking boys right now. Even if boys still make you think "Ewww . . . gross!" you may have a friend or two (or three or four) who are completely and totally boy crazy. You know, the girls whose lives center on what *he* said, or how *he* looked, or the way *he* smiled. They just can't stop talking about the boys in your class. . . .

When I say "boy crazy," I'm not talking about the girl who has noticed boys and makes a comment every now and then. I'm talking about the girl who talks and thinks about boys all. the. time. Do you know someone like that? I bet you do. It can get on your nerves after a while, especially if you haven't really thought a lot about boys yet (except for the fact that they can be really annoying).

When I was your age, I was seriously boy crazy. Over-the-top boy crazy. I don't know if some girls are jut born more boy crazy than others, but if so, then I was one of them. I always picked out the "cute boys" in my class the first week of school each year. I even put a note on a guy's desk in the fourth grade! In the note, I told him I liked him and asked him who he liked. Yeah, I know—pretty bold, huh? He told one of my friends he liked me, but we hardly talked for the rest of the year. It didn't matter. It was fun just knowing he liked me. My boy-crazy days didn't end in fourth grade. I had my eye

> He is WAY cute.
> Who do you think he likes?
> Do you think he's
> looking at me?

on another boy in fifth grade and in sixth grade, and . . . well, you get the picture.

You might wonder what the big deal is about boys. For some girls, they might not feel important unless a guy likes them and gives them attention. As they get older, these girls can focus on guys so much that they ignore other important things in their lives like their friends, schoolwork, and their relationship with God. There is a Bible verse every girl should memorize—boy crazy or not. Proverbs 4:23 says, "Guard your heart above all else, for it is the source of life." Even now, it is important for you to "guard your heart" from things that might take God's place there—things like boys. Even when you grow up and get married, you should love God more than anything or anyone else in the world. Girls who are boy crazy at an early age sometimes grow up and let a guy's love become more important than God's love. And those girls end up with broken hearts.

If one of your friends is going through a boy-crazy stage, you can't make her change, but don't give up on her. Be patient. She will probably come out of the fog eventually. When the time is right (*not* in front of all your friends), tell her (kindly) that you are worried about her spending so much time thinking about boys. She might listen—and she might not. And if you happen to be the boy-crazy one in this story, remember this: there is no hurry. Take it from me—someone who was way too boy crazy, way too young. You have *plenty* of years ahead of you to think about boys. Enjoy being young. Spend time with your friends. Work on your hobbies. Try out for the basketball team. Do what *you* want to do, and don't worry about what a guy thinks. (Most of the time, he's thinking about food, bodily noises, and getting to the next level on his video game.)

The truth is, only one guy is worth your time and full attention—Jesus Christ. Ask Him to help you understand how much He loves you. Ask Jesus to help you see the ways He shows His love toward you every day. When all other love fails (and it will), His love will never change. And that is something you can be totally crazy about.

The truth is, only one guy is worth your time and full attention—Jesus Christ.

What Real Friends Will Do for You

by Whitney Prosperi

One afternoon when I was in college, my friend Tammy and I went to the grocery store. Before we even began our trip, we started goofing around, and things began to get a little crazy. Before long, we were racing down the aisles with our shopping cart. (That's not a good idea, by the way.)

When Tammy got some speed going, she jumped up on the metal rail under the front of the cart and started to coast—or tried to. Here's a tip for free: make sure the cart can hold your weight. The end of the cart tipped up, and Tammy fell headfirst into the basket. The shopping cart (with her inside it) turned upside-down and flew toward the meat counter.

Honestly, it was one of the funniest things I have seen. Ever. And also the scariest. But she and the lunchmeat survived. Her hands were cut and bruised from the shopping cart. But her pride hurt worse.

While I was helping her climb out of the shopping cart and stand up, we noticed one of our other friends a few aisles away. She was staring at us like we were nuts. We waved at her. But she didn't wave back. She acted as if she didn't see us, turned around, and walked the other way. She was too ashamed to talk to us.

Has that ever happened to you? Did you ever think someone was your friend, but when you did something embarrassing or something she didn't like, she dumped you and turned the other way? We've all been there. It's much worse than bruised hands from a shopping cart.

Real friends are hard to find, but when you discover one, you have received one of God's best gifts. How do you know if you've got an authentic, stick-with-you-through-it-all kind of friend?

A genuine friend:
Sticks with you.

Everyone wants to be your friend when you have a party coming up or you get an extra ticket to the concert everybody wants to see. But what if you trip in the lunchroom? Or sit with the kid no one wants to sit with at lunch? Will your friend support you? Or will she turn on you? A true friend sticks with you. Even if you have toilet paper stuck to the bottom of your shoe. In fact, a real friend will tell you it's there before anyone notices.

What's the most important thing you look for in a friend?

Scan for Video Answers!

Keeps a secret.

Ever had a friend who couldn't keep her mouth shut? Ten seconds after you tell her something, she tells a gazillion other people. Before you know it, everyone knows your personal, private stuff. Trust is a must in real, I-can-count-on-you friendships. Ask God to bring you a friend who can—and will—keep things to herself.

Chooses what's right.

A true friend won't ask you to bail on what you believe. She won't ask you to do things that go against the Bible or God. She will help you make wise choices rather than pressure you to make foolish ones. She will choose what's right rather than what's popular. For example, dressing appropriately isn't always popular—but it's the right thing to do. This kind of friend is crucial because you become like the people you spend time with.

Points you toward God.

The best kind of friend challenges you to follow God. She knows that you'll be happiest and most fulfilled when you're trying to live the way God wants you to.

She will pray for you and remind you to put God first—instead of her! This kind of friend will help you stay on track and cheer you on when it comes to your faith.

What about you? Take a second to think about the kind of friend you are. Do you stick by your friends? Do you keep their secrets? Do you encourage them to do the right thing? Can they trust you to keep your word? Remember what your mom always told you: you have to be a friend to have a friend. Becoming the kind of friend you want to find is a good place to start.

A friend loves at all times.
—Proverbs 17:17

Whoever conceals an offense promotes love, but whoever gossips about it separates friends.—Proverbs 17:9

The one who walks with the wise will become wise.—Proverbs 13:20

Iron sharpens iron, and one man sharpens another.—Proverbs 27:17

WARNING→

Dangerous Friend Ahead

by Vicki Courtney

Warning: Too much time spent with these types of friends can be dangerous to your health:

The Joker

This person likes to say things that are mean and hurtful and then covers them by saying, "Just kidding!"

The Whisperer

This person always knows the latest scoop and is willing to share it to a listening ear.

The Boxer

This person loves a good fight—so much so that she looks for ways to start one just for the sake of drama.

As you read these descriptions, some of the girls (and guys!) you know may have popped into your head. Or maybe you saw yourself. We've all probably been guilty of being one of those kinds of friends.

Match the below symptoms with one of the following types of friends:

J = Joker   W = Whisperer   B = Boxer

___ Hey, did you hear about . . . but don't tell anyone I told you!

___ Nice swimsuit. I had one like that when I was five years old. Just kidding!

___ Her mom told my mom and my mom told me, but don't tell anyone.

___ I hate her! She's always starting drama!

___ Well, at least I didn't totally bomb on the test like you! Only kidding.

___ She makes me so mad. Let's tell everyone to ignore her at lunch.

___ Oooh, nice haircut! Don't worry, it'll grow out! JK!

___ I am not inviting her to my party. That'll show her. We should all talk about the party in front of her just to make her mad.

___ Ellie told me that Kate told her that she likes him. I hope he finds out. But don't tell anyone I told you.

Hopefully that matching game gave you a better idea of how to spot dangerous friendships. Remember, we've all probably been guilty of behaving like a Joker, Whisperer, or Boxer at some point. If a friend acts that way all the time, beware: she may turn and act that way toward you!

If you're prone to be a Joker, Whisperer, or Boxer, you can still change. Ask God to help you see when you treat someone badly. Apologize when you hurt someone. And when all else fails, just keep your mouth closed. Remember, "If you talk a lot, you are sure to sin; if you are wise, you will keep quiet" (Proverbs 10:19 NCV).

Extra Credit

1. Read Proverbs 26:18–19. Circle the type of friend it describes: Joker   Whisperer   Boxer
2. Read Proverbs 26:20. Circle the type of friend it describes: Joker   Whisperer   Boxer
3. Read Proverbs 26:21. Circle the type of friend it describes: Joker   Whisperer   Boxer

Quiz: What Kind of Friend Are You?

Take the quiz below to find out the kind of friend you are.

1. Being a friend means . . .

A) being kind to others no matter who they are.

B) being there for people you know and like.

C) being with people who can help your social status.

2. If your friends started talking badly about someone outside of your circle of friends, you would . . .

A) stand up for the person or walk away.

B) change the subject or keep quiet.

C) add your own comments.

3. A new girl in your grade does not have anyone to eat with at lunch, so you . . .

A) have her join you and your friends.

B) tell her that you should do lunch together one day.

C) trust that she will find her own way.

4. One of your friends is staying the night at your house, and your little sister asks you to play, so you . . .

A) ask your friend if you both can play one game with your sister.

B) tell your sister you'll play after your friend leaves.

C) tell your sister to get lost in front of your friend.

5. One of your friends shares with you in confidence who she likes, so you . . .

A) keep the information to yourself.

B) tell another close friend who can also keep a secret.

C) tell the guy that your friend likes him.

Total up your answers. How many A's, B's, and C's did you have?

Mostly A: You are a loyal friend. You are not afraid to go against the flow to be a good friend to others (even if they are different than you). You are true to yourself and do not allow others' opinions to shape your decisions.

Mostly B: You want the best of both worlds. You want to keep your values and your social status. Although you aren't too easily influenced, you haven't made up your mind completely about following the crowd.

Mostly C: You are more concerned about yourself than other people. You care more about how you appear to others rather than caring for others. Following the crowd too closely will give you the wrong reputation and will eventually lead to trouble. It's time to take some bold steps toward looking out for others.

10 tips

for Surviving Mean Girls (and How Not to Become One!)

by Vicki Courtney

Mean girls. They're probably the worst part of being a girl. If you don't believe me, just have a sleepover and invite an uneven number of girls. Throw in some popcorn and a little gossip, and you've got yourself a show—or better yet, a showdown. Mean girls are nothing new. Ask your mom—I bet she can share a story or two about mean girls she faced when she was your age. And some of us might have the courage to admit to being a mean girl from time to time. So, whether you know one or you are one, check out these ten bits of info:

1. You are who you hang with.

Take a look at 1 Corinthians 15:33: "Do not be misled: 'Bad company corrupts good character'" (NIV). If you hang out with girls who gossip, talk ugly about others, and leave people out on purpose, then you have probably been called a "mean girl" at your school. Choose your friends wisely. If you want to avoid a mean girl label, don't hang with girls who have made bullying their favorite hobby.

2. Use the "duck and dodge" maneuver.

If you are the victim of a mean girl, try to avoid her. Don't even give her a minute of your time and energy. If you see her coming, go another direction. And if you cannot avoid her, treat her as though she is invisible. Mean girls will usually move on to someone else if they don't get the response from you they are hoping for.

3. Pray for the mean girls and bullies.

The Bible tells us to "pray for those who mistreat you" (Luke 6:28 NIV). Yikes. What a tough command. That's the last thing you want to do. Yet something special happens when you pray for mean girls. You will begin to see them from a different perspective. You might even develop a little compassion for them. The next time someone is mean to you, say a prayer for her. Chances are, she needs it.

4. Keep your circle open.

Most girls will be drawn to other girls who share similar interests. This is normal, and there is nothing wrong with wanting to spend more time with girls you have more things in common with. This doesn't mean you can purposely leave someone out who's not in your same dance club or youth group at church. Try to be kind to everyone. Never close the door to new friendships. You may discover you have things in common with someone who is not in your friend group.

What is the best way to deal with mean girls?

Scan for Video Answers!

5. Be aware of the gossip machine.

If girls like to share gossip with you, don't take it as a compliment. They gossip with you because they know you will probably share your own gossip too. Simply change the subject as soon as you can, or say something like "I feel bad talking about her" and then change the subject to something safe—like say, boys! Remember, "the tongue has the power of life and death, and those who love it will eat its fruit" (Proverbs 18:21 NIV).

6. Beware of sharing news.

Remember that anyone who shares gossip *with* you will also gossip *about* you. Never tell a gossipy friend anything you don't want others to know, even if she's a close friend. If you are not getting along with her, what's to keep her from telling your secrets? You'll learn all too soon that "a gossip betrays a confidence, but a trustworthy person keeps a secret" (Proverbs 11:13 NIV).

27

7. Celebrate with your friends.

A true sign that a girl feels confident about herself is when she can be happy for others when they accomplish something. The next time a friend makes the team, make an effort to be happy for her—even when you feel sad if you didn't make the team. If you don't feel happy, act yourself into the feeling.

8. Consider the source.

People who make fun of others don't feel good about themselves. They somehow think that if they make fun of others, it will make them feel better about themselves and look cool to others. Sometimes the popular girls will be mean to others because they don't want anyone to take their place in the group. If they want to stay important, they think they have to make others look less popular.

9. Don't be a groupie.

A groupie is someone who feels like she MUST fit in with a certain group of friends. She doesn't want to be friends with anyone who isn't in "the" group. If the group has a mean-girl leader, many of the girls in the group will make bad choices just so they can "look cool" and stay in the group. Groupies are too insecure to stand up for what is right. If you are in a group like this, get out! Find new friends. Remember, "hate evil, love good" (Amos 5:15 NIV).

10. Find a sidekick.

Find at least one friend who also wants to be a nice girl. Agree to pray for each other. If you can't think of even one friend who is nice to others and who would be a good influence on you, ask God to lead you to one. In the meantime, ask yourself, "Why are my friends mean?" You might not like the answer.

Wise Words on Mean Girls (from Older Girls Who've Been There, Done That)

We surveyed girls your age and asked them what questions they had about growing up. Then we gave those questions to some high school girls who were happy to pass along their advice. Who better to answer those questions than girls who have been in your shoes? Here is one question you had along with the answers from girls who have been right where you are—and survived to tell about it!

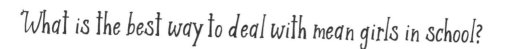

What is the best way to deal with mean girls in school?

The best way to deal with these girls is to kill them with kindness. I know it sounds cheesy, but when they look back, they will remember how nice you were to them. Maybe your actions will make them want to be different.—Cayla

Just be confident in who you are. If you can be confident and comfortable with who you are, the mean girls' comments and looks can't hurt you.—Sarah

For the most part, just try to ignore them. Chances are, if they see that their comments aren't affecting you, they'll stop. Also, try talking to a parent, a counselor, or someone you trust.—Kaitlyn

A lot of girls say mean things just to try to make themselves look better. Don't act like it bothers you, and then it won't be as fun for them. Oh, and one more thing—pray about it! God definitely cares about what upsets His daughters!—Stephanie

Mean girls are insecure and are willing to put down any other person to build themselves up. It is best just to ignore them and build up a true group of friends who will stick up for you when these insecure girls are brutal.—Alicia

What's the Big Deal with Having a Boyfriend?

by Vicki Courtney

"I want a boyfriend."

"If he would just talk to me . . ."

"He asked me to sit by him on the field trip!!"

Something about having a boyfriend makes you feel accepted. Wanted. Out of a sea of girls, he actually noticed *you*, liked you, and picked you. You are worth something to someone else (besides your parents, of course!). You are someone's girlfriend. And you have a boyfriend.

As I said earlier, I was *seriously* boy crazy when I was in school. My first official "boyfriend" came rather unexpectedly on the first day of fifth grade. A classmate sitting in the desk behind me tapped me on the shoulder and handed me a folded-up note. Before I mistakenly assumed that he was the sender, he quickly pointed to a cute boy with a shaggy haircut sitting a couple of desks behind him and whispered, "It's from him." I unfolded the note and read the following words: "I like you. Will you go with me? Circle YES or NO. From, Dorwin." (That's some name, isn't it?) I didn't know a thing about this guy except that he held the school record for the 100-yard dash. Sounded like good creds to me, so with little thought, I circled YES and passed back the note.

My heart skipped a beat when I glanced back and saw him open the note and flash that cool guy smile. We were officially "going steady." Don't laugh—that's what we called it back then. And back in the day, sometimes a guy would even give you a clunky silver ID bracelet with his name on it, a token of honor and admiration. I was awarded the ID bracelet on the second day of school, and voilà! I had a boyfriend.

He was the first in a long line of boyfriends. Throughout middle school and high school I almost always had a boyfriend. I never stopped to think that going from boyfriend to boyfriend was a problem. Lots of girls did it. At the time, I didn't understand that I had allowed a boyfriend to determine my worth. Having a boyfriend meant that I was pretty and cool and worth something. Not having a boyfriend meant that I was a loser. Or so I thought.

Funny thing though, even when I had a boyfriend, my heart never felt at peace. The initial flutter in my heart always wore off over time. That's because a guy can bring satisfaction temporarily, but he can never fulfill you or make you whole. Only God can do that.

I understand why being in a relationship didn't make me feel good inside. Exodus 34:14 says, "You must worship no other gods, for the Lord . . . is a God who is jealous about his relationship with you" (NLT). Did you catch that? God—the one who flung the stars in the sky and knows them each by name—is jealous about His relationship with you! You were created to love Him more than everyone and everything else; until you do,

your heart will never be fully satisfied. Not by money, a sense of humor, success in school, popularity, good looks, or even having a boyfriend. Having a boyfriend at the right time can bring satisfaction, but he is never supposed to give—or take away— your worth.

Fortunately, God stuck with me over the years. He patiently waited for me to let Him take the rightful place in my heart, a place that I had attempted to fill with a steady stream of boyfriends. When I was twenty-one, I finally gave my heart to Him, and my life has never been the same. I felt worth, value, and purpose in life. Who needs a silver ID bracelet when the God of this universe wants to inscribe His name on your heart?

10 Signs You Might Be Too Boy Crazy

* Your friends roll their eyes when you start talking about guys—again.

* Your journal is full of notes about all your crushes.

* You dress to get attention from your latest crush.

* You have a crush on more than one guy—at the same time.

* Guys are ALWAYS the topic of conversation with friends.

* You daydream about what it would be like to have a boy-friend (all. the. time.).

* You get crazy jealous when one of your friends talks about a boy you like.

* You stalk your crush (social media, in the halls at school, at his ballgames).

* You believe your life would be better if you had a boyfriend.

* You replace one crush with another immediately.

Sweet Stuff to Do with Your Friends

Make a Difference

- Organize a one-day sports camp for younger kids in your neighborhood.
- Make flyers and distribute them in your neighborhood offering your help with house or yard jobs.
- Visit an elderly neighbor, friend of your family, or family member.
- Clean out your closet, and donate the stuff you don't want or need to kids who need it.
- Make small gifts or baked goods and deliver them to your neighbors, teachers, or coaches for no reason.

Just for Fun

- Pack a lunch and have a picnic.
- Bake cookies.
- Write words of encouragement to each other in a special journal that you pass back and forth.
- Open a one-night restaurant (with menus and candles), and cook dinner for your parents or families.
- Camp out in the backyard.
- Organize a family game night.
- Learn some new card games.
- Put a puzzle together.
- Run through a sprinkler or get out your old Slip 'n Slide.
- Play in the summer rain (when it is not lightning!).

Get Creative

- Make photo books together (for yourselves or for your families) with your digital pictures.
- Start a band.
- Blow up balloons, put notes and candy inside, and give them to friends.
- Make a time capsule.
- Invent a new dance routine to your favorite song.
- Set up an obstacle course, and invite friends over for a contest.
- Take turns making up a scavenger hunt for each other with a prize at the end.
- Make a movie with your digital device.
- Make a magazine collage.
- Invent your own board game.
- Write a play, cast your friends in the roles, and then put the play on for your family.
- Redecorate your rooms together.
- Make up your own holiday and decide how you're going to celebrate it.
- Give each other manicures or pedicures.
- Take turns writing a story and see where it leads (don't discuss the plot).
- Pick a good book to read together.

The Bully

by Vicki Courtney

I recently asked girls your age to tell me about a time when another girl was mean to them. One girl named Shelby described an extremely hurtful event that happened when she was training for her very first horse show. She was riding her pony at the stables, and a girl who practiced at the same time began to taunt her and say some really mean things. The mean girl teased Shelby and said, "Your horse will never be show material." This became a pattern. Every time Shelby went to the stables to ride, the girl was ready with new words of hatred. She would also talk behind Shelby's back and tell the other girls at the stable that Shelby's family didn't have much money. She told them Shelby probably wouldn't be able to afford to show her horse much longer. This bully would brag to the other girls about how much longer she had been riding horses than Shelby and even told Shelby that she would "kick her rear end" if they showed their horses at the same show. She actually used a very bad word in the place of "rear end." You get the picture.

Shelby told her mother about the mean girl. Her mom encouraged her to try to ignore the mean girl's comments and not let this girl stand in the way of Shelby's goal. Shelby cried at first because all she wanted to do was fit in and have a good time. Her mom encouraged her to find new friends to ride with. And Shelby did just that. And guess what happened? Shelby won a Grand Champion ribbon with her pony! Sometimes she still sees the mean girl at the stables, but Shelby said, "I am always nice and kind to her. It makes me feel good to be nice to other people."

Proverbs 11:17 says, "A kind person benefits himself, but a cruel person brings himself trouble" (NET). When I read that verse, I think of Shelby and that mean girl at the stables. Shelby benefited by being kind. Just like a plant needs water (nourishment) to grow and be healthy, being kind to others can be like watering our souls to keep them healthy too. The mean girl, on the other hand, was only hurting herself by being mean. She thought she was hurting Shelby when she dished out her cruel comments. In the end, though, her plan backfired. She may not realize it, but little by little, that mean girl is destroying herself with every cruel remark she makes. In other words, she's really hurting herself by being mean!

The next time someone is mean to you, remember Shelby's story. It's hard to hold your head up high and be kind when someone is mean to you. But if you do, you will be helping yourself!

Quiz: Are You a Gossip Girl?

by Susan Palacio

Gossip is a big problem. In fact, chances are you've already experienced the negative effects of gossip. Someone shared your secrets; perhaps someone started a rumor about you; or maybe you joined in when someone started talking about another girl.

Gossip is a disease that can destroy friendships. Thankfully there is a cure: you! God can give you the strength to stop, but you have to first admit you have a problem and then ask for His help. Take the quiz on the next two pages to see how you measure up against gossip.

When your teacher was handing back the tests, you accidentally saw Brady's test grade—and it wasn't good. You actually did pretty well. Later that day, your friends begin talking about how hard the test was. You . . .

A) Agree with them and tell them what you made.

B) Agree with them and tell them about Brady's test grade!

You usually sit with the same group of friends at lunch. You notice that Kaitlyn hasn't really been eating her lunch the past few days. You . . .

A Keep quiet and later ask Kaitlyn in private if everything is okay.

B) Wait until Kaitlyn leaves the table and then ask your friends if they think she has an eating disorder.

At cheerleading practice, Emma shows up very late. She was pulled out of class earlier in the day and sent to the principal's office. You are sure there's a juicy story behind it. You . . .

A) Ask her about it after practice because you're worried about her.

B) Talk with your friends about all the possible reasons she could have been in trouble.

Walking down the hallway, you see one of your classmates trip and fall flat on his face. He wasn't hurt, but you thought it was hilarious. You walk back to class and sit down next to one of your friends. You . . .

A) Resist the temptation to tell her and instead talk about something else.

B) Cover your laugh with your hand and immediately spill the story to your friend.

In the bathroom, you overhear Hayley and Taylor talking about how they think Hayden is the cutest guy in school. You return to class and sit next to your best friend. You . . .

A) Say nothing because you wouldn't want someone else talking about your crushes.

B) Text your friend, detailing the conversation you just overheard. Friends tell friends everything, right?

Nicole tells you that her parents are getting divorced. It's kind of shocking because Nicole's mom is very involved as a volunteer at your school and her dad is a teacher there. The next time Nicole's mom volunteers in your class, you . . .

A) Remember what Nicole said and make a mental note to ask Nicole later how she's doing.

B) Lean over to your friend Maddie and whisper, "Did you hear that Nicole's mom and dad are getting a divorce?"

Over the weekend you hear that your friend Olivia got in trouble for texting a boy in the middle of the night. You . . .

A) Say nothing and do nothing. She already feels bad about it. Why make it worse?

B) Immediately text your best friend, "Remind me to tell you something about Olivia later!"

A girl in your grade suddenly transfers to another school. You and your friends are talking about why she left. You . . .

A) Say, "We don't know what happened" and immediately change the subject.

B) Go right alone with your friends and agree it was probably because she was struggling to keep her grades up.

How did you score?

Did you score mostly A's? If so, you're no gossip queen!

You understand the benefits of staying out of things that don't concern you! You try to keep information to yourself, even if you are dying to tell someone. You value being known as someone who does not participate in gossip, and you understand the negative effects it can have on friendships. Things might sometimes slip out, but you understand that it's not right. Keep a close watch when you start conversations with "Guess what I heard?" or "Did you hear . . . ?" Keep going in the right direction!

Did you score mostly B's? If so, you are the gossip queen! (P.S. That's not a good thing!)

If drama is going on, you usually have a major part in the show! Even though you try, you just can't resist asking questions to find out information about others. And sometimes you struggle with telling news or information that just isn't yours to tell. Take off that crown! You can control your tongue by not participating in gossip, no matter how tempting the situation is. Walk away from situations where you're listening to gossip, and practice holding your tongue by not sharing everything with your friends, even your BFF. In the end you'll develop healthy friendships that won't be torn apart by gossip!

Pssst, He Might Like You

by Pam Gibbs

How do you know if a guy likes you, like as a girlfriend? One minute he says something kind, and the next minute, he's teasing you about your hair. What's the deal? Here are some hints that *might* help you decide.

His actions speak for him.

Does he look you in the eye when he talks to you? Does he get clumsy when you are around? Does he stutter when he tries to talk to you? These are all non-verbal clues that he may like you.

He wants to be around you.

He will try to stand in line with you. He will try to sit by you in the cafeteria. He will "accidentally" bump into you in the hallway. He will choose a seat near you—often behind you so he can see you without you knowing it (he's embarrassed).

He will act goofy around you.

He may say, "Watch this!" and then do something completely daring or stupid—like jump off a wall or try a difficult trick on his bike. He may talk to you a lot one day and then ignore you the next.

He will want to help you—even when you don't need it.

He will open doors for you. He may ask if you need help with your homework (when he's the one who got the bad grade). Why? Because God created guys to want to be protectors, to be strong and respected. He thinks that you will like that he cares about you. And that's a good thing.

He asks you questions—even goofy ones.

Do you like _____ (insert name of band)? What's in your lunch? You going to the game this weekend? Asking questions does two things: it helps him get to know you, and it gives him an excuse to keep talking to you (see previous paragraph).

You talk a lot together.

This will happen more and more as you get older. On the phone or in a text, you will talk about the day, who got in trouble, and how confusing your math teacher is. You will talk about weekend plans and the coolest new techie gadget—everyday stuff.

He teases you.

He'll pull your hair (gently). He will make fun of your shoes. He will lightly slug you in the arm. He will make fun of your swing or your jump shot. All of these are just ways to disguise the fact that he likes you.

His friends tease him.

If he is caught talking to you, you can be sure that his friends will tease him in some way. You may not see it every time (or any time), but they will. If he really, really likes you, he won't mind getting teased. It's sort of an honor. Being teased because a girl talks to him is better than a girl not noticing him.

He tries to make you laugh.

He'll make stupid jokes. He'll make fun of himself. He'll joke around with the girl in line in front of you. He wants to make you laugh. To him, that's a sign that you like him.

One more thing:

These signs are no guarantees. Some guys tease you because they are immature. Other guys are just naturally clumsy. There are some mysteries that just aren't easily solved. And the minds of guys are a mystery that may never be completely unraveled.

Being There:
How to Help a Hurting Friend

by Pam Gibbs

It's Monday morning, and you got to school early. You're hanging out at the lockers when you see your best friend walk through the front door. Immediately, you know something is horribly wrong. Her shoulders are slumped. She won't make eye contact. She looks like she has been crying. You slam your locker door and run over so you can talk to her before anyone else realizes she's there.

"My parents told me last night that they're getting a divorce."

Wow. Talk about unexpected. Her parents seemed so cool when you were at her house.

You mumble something stupid (you think) and say you're sorry. Nothing else pops into your brain. You wish you could say or do something to help her feel better.

Chances are, you've been in a situation like this. The topic may not have been divorce. It could be a jillion other things—a friend's sister gets pregnant. Or a friend's dad has cancer. Your bestie's dog got run over. Bad stuff happens, even to your friends. How can you help?

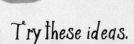

Try these ideas.

Listen.

Your friend will need a safe place to vent. She will need someone who can handle her emotions—anger, hurt, confusion, sadness, fear, worry. You don't have to fix the situation—and you probably can't, even if you wanted to. Just let your friend talk it out without judging her. She needs to know you have her back and support her.

Be there.

If a friend loses a loved one or a pet, there are no words to make her feel better. But you can be there. Just be there. Physically. Go to her house and just hang out with her. You don't even have to talk about the death (or the divorce or whatever is making her sad). Just be yourself, and let her be herself. She may start talking about what's going on. If she does, just listen (remember idea #1?). She may just want to talk about your latest crush or homework. That's okay too. Let her decide how the day will go.

Ask.

If you are not sure how you can help, ask your friend. She may be able to tell you what she needs. Then again, she may not have a clue. If she can't think of anything, then tell her that when she *does* know what she needs—like a ride to school or someone to go to the funeral home with her—she can totally ask you, and you'll do whatever you can to help.

Help.

You may think of ways you can help, like inviting her over for a slumber party or helping her address cards or even going to the hospital with her. When you are sure of ways you can make the situation better, then just do it. If you're not sure, ask your mom and dad what they think of your idea. They might have some information that you don't, so their input can be helpful. You might also ask yourself, "What would I want or need if that happened to me?" Then decide if your friend would want the same things. If so, then you know how you can help.

Encourage.

Your friend will need some encouraging words. Make her a card. Send her texts once in a while. Use a funny joke you share as a way to lift her spirits. Let her know you think she can handle whatever she is facing. Remind her that God has not forgotten her (He hasn't!) and that He loves her deeply (He does!). Let her know you are praying for her.

Carry one another's burdens; in this way you will fulfill the law of Christ.
—Galatians 6:2

Rejoice with those who rejoice; weep with those who weep.
—Romans 12:15

Green~Tinted Glasses:
Looking at Life through the Lens of Jealousy

by Pam Gibbs

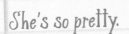

She's so pretty.

I wish I were as tall as she is.

Why can't I be as good at soccer as she is?

She's good at everything.

She never makes a bad grade.

Why doesn't my hair look like that?

I wish I could be as popular as she is.

I wish I had all the cool stuff she has.

Do those thoughts ever sneak into your head? Maybe late at night when the TV is off and the house is quiet? You're thinking about your day, and WHAM! You remember that girl at the basketball game—the one with talent you'll never have. Then you start thinking about the girl in your science class, the one who always makes straight A's. Why can't you ever do as well? You try just as hard. And then you think about that girl who always has cool clothes or the girl who can talk to guys with confidence. It's just not fair.

Jealousy creeps in like that. A thought here. A comment there. Before you know it, your jealousy turns into resentment. And if you don't stop that train of thought, you're on your way to Enemy Land faster than you can say "envy."

Have you ever heard the saying, "Green with envy"? Think of jealousy like wearing a pair of green-tinted glasses. Everywhere you look, things will look green. The sky. The walls. Your sister. Your dog. All green. Of course, you know that's not reality—the glasses distorted your vision. The same applies to jealousy. What you are thinking in that moment ("I hate my life") isn't true—but the jealousy distorts your perspective.

How do you curb jealousy? How do you tame your thoughts so that you don't always feel like you don't measure up? Here are a few ideas.

Find the source.

When jealous thoughts pop into your head, stop and ask yourself one question: Why are you jealous of _____? When you get that answer (she's more popular), ask the question again: Why are you jealous that she's more popular? (more people like her). Ask it again: Why are you jealous that more people like her? (because I don't think people like me). Jackpot! That's the real reason you're jealous.

Try it yourself:
Why am I jealous of
_____?
Why am I jealous that she
_____?
Why are you jealous that
_____?

Did you find your answer? This little test doesn't work for every situation. Most of the time it will get to the root of your jealousy.

Take a closer look.

Before you get caught up in jealousy over what another girl has or can do, take a closer look at that person's life. What do you think it's like to live in her soccer cleats? Do you want to put in all the hours of practice she does? Are you committed to play in the weather—even if it's 55 degrees and pouring down rain? Would you be willing to give up time with friends to go to all the games? Are you okay with doing your homework after a game—at eleven p.m. at night?

When you stop to think about another person's life, sometimes you don't get so jealous. What price does a girl pay to be popular? Can she ever be sure she is liked for who she is, or just because she's popular? What is it *really* like to be a straight A student? What pressure does she feel to be perfect?

Take inventory.

At its heart, jealousy isn't about another person. It's about *you*. What you own or don't own. What you can do or can't do. How you measure up to those around you. Are you as pretty? Liked? Smart? Tall? Short? Skinny? Popular? Funny? This comparison game messes with your ability to recognize you own gifts and abilities. You will never be free of jealousy's grasp until you stop looking at everyone else and start looking at all the blessings around you. Your health. Your family. Your sense of humor. Your ability to sympathize with others. Jealousy will control your life until you can become okay with how God made you and how God has blessed you. The Bible calls that *contentment*.

Being content doesn't mean that you don't try your best in school or that you stop taking care of your body and your clothes. Contentment means that you know that grades and clothes and popularity and looks don't define you. Clothes are nice, but they don't last. The same goes for popularity. Being content means knowing that no matter what happens, God loves you and has a plan for your life even now as a tween.

When you look through that lens, your life looks a whole lot brighter.

Your Mouth

As girls, we are so concerned with how we look and what others think about us that we miss the most important aspect of our appearance and reputation—our mouths! Our words, or our "tongues" as Scripture calls them, control our mouths. Take a look at the verses below that have to do with the mouth, and then take a look into your heart as you answer the questions below.

The one who guards [her] mouth protects [her] life; the one who opens [her] lips invites [her] own ruin.—Proverbs 13:3

- What is the outcome for the person who does not watch her words?

  _____

- What are some ways you have seen ruin come to your life or another's life through unnecessarily spoken words?

  _____

- How can watching what you say actually protect your life?

  _____

When there are many words, sin is unavoidable, but the one who controls [her] lips is wise.—Proverbs 10:19

- What trails right behind too many words? When have you seen your sin in connection with something that you said?

  _____

- What does this verse call the person who controls her lips?

  _____

- What would it look like for you to control your lips?

_____

With [her] mouth the ungodly destroys [her] neighbor, but through knowledge the righteous are rescued.—Proverbs 11:9

- Does *neighbor* mean just those people who live in your neighborhood? (Hint: Nope. Your neighbor is anyone God puts in your life.)

_____

- How have you recently destroyed someone with your words?

_____

- What does this proverb call the person who destroys another with her words?

_____

Think about the people you are prone to talk about. Do you really know any of them? Do you know what is going on in their lives? Do you know about their struggles, their insecurities, their home lives?

If you were able to name how you destroyed someone with your words, then that's proof that you probably need to ask Jesus to help you control your lips. He can help you keep your words in check and make your mouth one of your greatest features!

You're Not Invited!
What to Do When You Get Left Out

by *Susie Davis and Pam Gibbs*

Every Valentine's Day was the same. Either you brought a valentine for everyone in the class or you didn't bring any at all. That was the rule at my elementary school. The teachers made that rule so kids wouldn't get their feelings hurt by being left out. That rule also applied to invitations to birthday parties—either you bring an invitation to everyone in the class or you have to mail them.

But what about now? Those rules don't apply anymore. Whether they're paper, text, or e-mail, invitations now fly right and left for parties your classmates have throughout the school year. Sometimes you're invited, and sometimes you're not. Even if you're not good friends with the birthday girl, you still feel hurt when you hear about a party you didn't get invited to.

It happens something like this: You're in the cafeteria at school, and you just got your tray of food. As you head toward the table where all your friends are sitting, from a distance you can see they are all laughing and having fun. But just when you get close to the table and start to put your tray down, you hear a friend say under her breath, "Shhhh! She's not invited." And then the table talk stops, and everyone looks up at you. It's the worst feeling.

So what's a girl to do when she gets left out? After all, it happens to every girl at some point. How do you hold your head up when you feel like someone has kicked you in the stomach by excluding you? How do you handle your feelings when you know that someone didn't like you enough to invite you? And what do you do *after* the party when your friends talk about what a great time they had?

What's a girl to do?

When you get left out, your feelings get hurt. That's normal. And when your feelings get hurt, sometimes you get angry— angry at the person who left you out and sometimes even angry at your friends who got invited. When that happens, you may want to say ugly things about the girl or give her a bad look at school. That's really not the best idea because hurting others only creates more problems. When the time comes and you find yourself left out, here are a few helpful hints:

Admit how you feel.

Being left out hurts. Go ahead and say that out loud to someone you trust. Maybe tell your mom or your best friend that not being invited to a party hurts. When you talk about how you feel, the feelings don't feel as strong as if you hide them or keep them to yourself.

Remember that you're not alone.

There are dozens of reasons why you might not have been invited, and those reasons don't mean that you are not a fabulous person. Lots of fabulous people aren't invited to parties! And in this case, you are the fabulous person who wasn't invited. Don't let being left out ruin the way you feel about yourself.

Do something else.

Don't just sit around thinking about being left out. Instead, create a new plan. Look over the suggestions listed on the next page in "What to Do When You're Not Invited," and pick out a few you could try. And invite some people to join you. You'll be much less sad if you have a great time too!

Forgive the person who hurt your feelings.

Don't hold a grudge against her. Don't stay angry at her. The person giving the party might not have done anything wrong by not inviting you (you don't invite *everybody* to your parties, do you?). I found a verse that helps me in this kind of situation; it's Colossians 3:13, and it says, "Put up with each other, and forgive anyone who does you wrong, just as Christ has forgiven you" (CEV). We need to forgive because Christ always forgives us. It's a great verse to memorize. After you get that one tucked in your heart, remember to pray that God will help you get over the hurt feelings. He wants to help you. He is very interested in being invited to help you with your everyday life!

49

What to Do When You're Not Invited

1. Invite a new friend over, and take the chance to get to know someone you don't know well.

2. Ask your mom to take you to a local craft store the day of the party, and try out a new hobby.

3. Check out a book at the library that you've been dying to read. Then make a big bowl of popcorn and jump into the new story.

4. Gather a few of your neighborhood friends (even if they aren't in your grade) and surprise a few of your neighbors by raking leaves in their yard. Or ask permission to wash their cars. Have fun serving someone who lives close by.

5. Ask your dad or mom on a date. They might even be willing to take you to dinner or to a movie you have been wanting to see.

6. Call your grandparents and catch up on the phone with them. Or create a card for them and tell them about what's going on in your life.

7. Here's the last idea—and it might be a hard one to do: Make a gift or card for the person who excluded you from the party. Ask God for courage to do this, and only do it if you can have the right attitude. Sometimes blessing someone who has hurt you (whether she meant to or not) can be the biggest blessing of all!

NEVER EVERs
About Relationships

NEVER EVER say ugly things about people and think it will turn out well.

NEVER EVER ignore your friends just to get a boy to notice you.

NEVER EVER lie to your parents.

NEVER EVER yell at your siblings and tell them you hate them.

NEVER EVER forget to treat others as you would like to be treated.

NEVER EVER forget to thank people who take care of you.

NEVER EVER make your friends look stupid so you can look smart.

NEVER EVER do something you know is wrong just to fit in with the crowd.

NEVER EVER think you're being a baby if you need your parents to help you out.

NEVER EVER forget that gossip breaks up friendships.

How to Talk to a Boy

by Pam Gibbs

When you were six, boys had the cooties. Now boys are cute. You used to avoid them in the hallways. Now you want to sit next to them in class. Once you didn't care if you talked to one ever again. Now you can't figure out how to talk to them at all. Somewhere there ought to be a manual for how to talk to a boy, like the manual for working the TV your parents just bought. Unfortunately, such a manual doesn't exist. Talking to boys is really not much different than talking to girls, especially since the main goal should be building a friendship. Right?! Here are a few tips to get you started:

Act confident.

Some girls get nervous at the thought of talking to boys. Believe it or not, that's normal. Even though you *feel* scared, *act* like you're not. Hold your head up. Look him in the eye. Fake your way into actually being confident.

Use good body language.

Turn your body toward him, not away from him. Don't constantly look at the floor or your nails or that piece of hair that keeps bugging you. Smile. Again, hold your head up and your shoulders back. Don't slouch in your chair or keep your arms crossed.

Be patient.

If a boy doesn't really say much back to you at first, give him time. He might be trying to stir up the courage to risk talking to you. If he does talk to you, don't go crazy on him. Don't "accidentally" see him in the hall or text him all the time. Boys don't like pushy girls. Remember, the goal is to be his friend, not some crazed stalker.

Ask him questions.

The best way to start a conversation with a boy is to ask a question. How did you do on the test? What did you do on summer vacation? Find out what he likes—Pepsi versus Coke. Favorite color. Favorite band. Sports he loves to watch but can't play. You get the idea.

Ask more about his favorite hobby.

Everybody has that one thing they love. For boys, it could be a particular sport (or lots of them), computers, cars, or even something you've never heard of before. Whatever it is, ask him more details about it. Chances are you won't know a whole lot. This gives him the opportunity to share about the things that matter to him most.

Give him a chance to answer.

If you ask him questions, don't give your opinion and ideas without letting him explain his answer first. When you are nervous, you might accidentally start talking over his answers in an effort to keep the conversation going. Listen before speaking. Listen more than you speak. If you don't understand something or if his answer sparks a new question, that's great. Just give him a chance to finish his first thought before jumping to the next one.

Be yourself.

Don't act like you know everything about sports if you don't. Don't act like you're a dumb blonde when your grades are in the top ten percent. Don't hide your love of french fries with ranch dressing. Don't act like the kind of girl you think he would like. You can spot a fake a mile away— and so can he. If he doesn't like you as you are, then your friendship won't go anywhere, and that's okay. That's part of learning what relationships are all about. Besides, being a fake takes way too much energy.

Honor your parents' boundaries about talking to and texting boys.

If they do not want you to text boys then explain that to your guy friends if they happen to text you.

I Don't Mean to Brag, but . . .

by Vicki Courtney

One afternoon my daughter (who was in high school then) and I stepped into a Christian bookstore near our house to take a look around. Actually, I wanted to see if the bookstore was selling a new book I had just written. I told my daughter, "Shh . . . we're just checking to see if it's on the shelves, but don't say anything about me being an author." It was like we were on a secret mission. Sneak in. Look around. Sneak out. We headed to the section where the book would be—and there it was! I gave my daughter a silent thumbs up, and she smiled. Even though I had a copy at home, I picked up the book and began thumbing through the pages while my daughter looked at some other stuff in the store.

In a flash, the store manager appeared by my side. He noticed the book and said, "You know, that book is written by a local author who lives right here in town." I could sense my daughter cracking up right beside me, so I shot her a warning glare. (You know the kind I'm talking about!) Then the manager continued, "In fact, she has written quite a few books that your daughter might enjoy." No way. Please tell me he did not just say that. At that point I didn't have to look at my daughter. I knew she was cracking up. In fact, she was so tickled that she walked around the corner to hide her face and finish off her little laugh-fest.

I acted very interested in what the manager was telling me and thanked him for the advice, but I didn't tell him I was the author. And besides, how do I explain thumbing through my own book? Yikes! After he walked away, I rounded the corner to look for my daughter. She was doubled over laughing and asked between gasps: "Mom, why didn't you tell him you were the author?"

The truth is, I didn't want the manager to think I was bragging. At that point I grabbed her hand and told her it was time to head out before she blew our cover.

Why Do We Brag?

Let's get real. Everybody is tempted to brag. It's difficult to resist the urge to put the spotlight on ourselves sometimes. But why? Sometimes, we want other people to like us. We want our friends to think we're cool. Or perhaps we brag because we feel insecure. Most girls struggle with feeling unsure of themselves at this age. And sometimes we brag because we are just super-excited about something cool we have worked at to accomplish—like earning that grade or making the soccer team.

When Does It Become Bragging?

Sure, we want people to like us. And of course you want to share good news with your friends. That's completely normal. So how do you know when you've crossed the line into bragging? Here are a few possibilities:

- When you keep talking about it over and over and over and . . .
- When you tell a girl something cool about you just to make her feel bad
- When you start praising yourself, such as saying, "I *am* the best player on the team, aren't I?" or "He sooo likes me."
- When you begin a sentence with, "I don't mean to brag, but . . . "

- When you want to share something just to impress other people
- When friends roll their eyes when you start to talk about yourself

Pray and ask God to help you hold your tongue when you're tempted to brag. Besides, a compliment is always sweeter when it comes from someone else!

Let someone else praise you, and not your own mouth; an outsider, and not your own lips.
—Proverbs 27:2 NIV

The crucible for silver and the furnace for gold, but people are tested by their praise.
—Proverbs 27:21 NIV

Are You a GOOD Friend?

by Susan Palacio

Finish these stories to find out if you're a good friend!

Story #1

One day you decide you want to go to the _____ (place). Knowing you need Mom's

okay, you call out, "Mom, can you PLEEEEEEEEEASE take me to the _____

(same place)." Because your mom is so _____ (positive adjective), she

of course says, "Sure, honey." Thrilled she said yes, you immediately ask if you can invite

_____ (name of friend #1) to come along. Again, your mom says, "Sure."

So you call _____ (name of friend #1), and her mom agrees to let her go

with you. You are both so _____ (expressive adjective) because you've been

talking about wanting to go to _____ (same place) the whole week!

Then your phone rings. After fighting with _____ (your brother or sister) to

give your phone back to you, you answer and hear, "Hi, _____ (your name), it's

_____ (friend #2). You'll never guess where I'm going! My mom is taking me

to _____ (place #2 you have dreamed about going), and I'm allowed to invite

one friend! Do you want to go?" You can't believe it! You've *always* wanted to go there.

Then you remember your conversation with _____ (friend #1). You respond to

_____ (friend #2) and say, "_____" (your decision to go with

friend #1 or friend #2).

Story #2

School is about to start and you feel _____ (adjective). Your friend from

_____ (place you go every week) has just moved to a new house and now

goes to your school! You are _____ (good adjective) because she is really

sweet. Her name is _____ (name of first girl).

 Your friends from school, _____ (name of second girl),

_____ (name of third girl), and _____ (name of fourth

girl) are the popular girls. They aren't really _____ (negative adjective),

but they don't really want new friends either.

 At lunchtime on the first day of school, you sit with _____

(name of first girl). After lunch, you are talking with the popular girls when they say that

_____ (name of first girl) is _____ (expressive adverb)

_____ (mean adjective) and ask you why you were sitting with her.

You don't know whether to agree with them (they are your friends after all), or stick up for

your other friend. After thinking for a second, you say, "_____

_____" (reaction to something mean that was said).

The next day at lunch, you sit with _____ (first girl, popular girls, or both).

Turn the page to see how you scored!

How did you do?

Story #1: Did you spend the day with friend #1 or friend #2?

If you answered friend #1, congratulations! You are a good friend. You are faithful and understand the importance of keeping your word. Even if "something better" comes along, you will not ditch a friend.

If you answered friend #2, you may need to rethink the way you handle friendships. If you were the first friend, how would you feel if someone cancelled plans with you to do something else with another friend? Always remember to think of everyone involved when making a decision like this. It can be tempting to change your mind if given an option that sounds like more fun. If you do, though, your friends may begin to lose their trust in you.

Story #2: How did your story end?

If you stuck up for your friend who was new to school, you are a good friend! You are not tempted to gossip, and you are not afraid to stand up for someone, even if it means your other friends may not accept you. You understand that it is important to treat everyone with respect. You either chose to sit with her the next day at lunch or you arranged for all your friends to sit together!

If you either agreed with the girls or didn't say anything, you have some work to do! Start by looking at the type of friends you have. If your school friends are willing to say ugly things about someone else, how do you know they wouldn't someday say ugly stuff about you? I know it can be hard to do the right thing, especially if your friends are doing the wrong thing, but a true friend will stand up for you.

Best Friends Not~So~Forever

by Pam Gibbs

You met on the first day of kindergarten on Ms. Simpson's ABC rug. You were instantly inseparable. You rode bikes together, went to the library together, and even lost teeth at the same time. You bunked together at summer camp and fell in the lake when you both tried canoeing at the same time. You can finish each other's sentences and can even tell when something is wrong without a word being said. But now, something has changed. She doesn't want to spend as much time with you. When you hang out, she seems distracted and preoccupied. Being around her is different, but you can't quite figure out what has changed.

Until you see her at the ball field while watching your little brother's game.

She is at the concession stand hanging out with the new girl in school. Your friend has a big smile plastered on her face and is laughing so hard that she is grabbing her sides.

Mystery solved. Your BFF has a new BFF.

Now what?

Losing a best friend is never easy. And unfortunately, most girls your age lose their best friend at some point. Although you may be tempted to lash out in disappointment and anger, hurting her back won't make you feel any better in the long run. Instead, try these suggestions for dealing with your changing friendships. Some of them might not apply to you, but some could make the transition a little less painful.

Own your feelings.

When your BFF becomes best friends with someone else, you feel like you've been kicked in the gut. You feel betrayed. Left behind. Abandoned. Rejected. You are *supposed* to feel that way. Denying that you have been hurt won't make you feel any better; those feelings won't go away just because you try to forget them. Explain how you feel to a friend, your mom, your big sister, or even your teddy bear. Being honest with how you feel eases the sting.

Talk to her.

Tell your BFF how you feel—but be careful about what you say and how you say it. Saying "You never hang out with me anymore!" or "You don't care about our friendship anymore!" is probably not going to patch things up. Say something like, "I'm sad that we don't hang out as much any more" or "I feel like we aren't as close as we used to be. Do you think we are?" This will open the door to discussion. Your lack of closeness may not have anything to do with you. She may be struggling with something. Be prepared for her to share that she wants to spend time with lots of different people. She may be changing, and that could change your friendship.

Don't be super clingy.

When your best friend begins to pull away, the worst response is to get super needy or to go into clingy mode. Demanding her undivided attention and complete loyalty will backfire and push her even further away. Give her some distance and some time. She may eventually try to bridge the gap between you two—or she might not. Either way, being clingy doesn't help.

Keep your jealousy in check.

Jealousy can make you do stupid things—like saying something mean on social media or sending a horrible text message. Ask yourself where the jealousy is coming from. Are you afraid of being alone? Are you afraid of not being popular? Sometimes jealousy can reveal your real motivation for being friends.

Don't start a battle of the besties.

If your best friend starts hanging out with other people, don't grab a needy girl, crown her your new BFF, and start a war with your old BFF. You've probably seen this happen at school. Stirring up girl drama with gossip and rumors and mean behavior will destroy any possibility of mending your friendship.

Consider hanging out with your BFF and her new friend.

Would you feel comfortable hanging out with your BFF and her new friend? You might not know until you try. There's no rule that says that all three of you can't be friends. But be careful that you don't end up feeling like the tagalong who gets ignored. A lot of times, when three girls get together, one girl feels left out.

Be patient.

Most new friendships are a little like getting a new phone or a new app. Hanging out with a new friend feels fun and interesting and exciting and adventurous. You want to spend all of your time with that person, learning all about her and her world and her perspective. But just like a new app, the "new" of the friendship wears off and you find a balance in your time and attention.

Be patient with your friend. The newness of that friendship will eventually fade, and she will learn how to balance her time and her friendships.

Develop other friendships.

This may be the perfect time for you to get to know that new girl at your church or that quiet girl on the team. Spending less time with your BFF may actually open the door for more friendships that can be lifelong and life-changing. But you'll never know if you don't take the time and take the chance.

Above all, remember this: your worth is not determined by whether or not you have a BFF or who that BFF is. Your worth has already been determined by the God who created the stars and calls them each by name. When He formed, molded, and shaped you, He did so with intent and purpose. And before He created you, He loved you (Ephesians 1:4–5). And no BFF can ever take that away.

Your worth is not determined by whether or not you have a BFF or who that BFF is.

Wise Words on Cliques

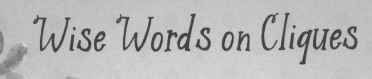

Everywhere you go, there will be cliques. Don't try to act like something you're not just to fit in with a clique. God will supply you with great friends if you just ask Him to.—Cayla

Cliques, oh goodness. The thing about cliques is just that everyone is so insecure and they can't handle not being the center of attention. Just find a good group of friends and stick with them; that way you're too busy having fun with your friends instead of dealing with the insecure girls that are in the cliques.—Sarah

Cliques will follow you wherever you go, even after middle school. Sadly, it's just a part of life. Just be yourself. True friends will love you for who you are and will stick with you through thick and thin.—Kaitlyn

Don't worry about having to be in the popular crowd. A lot of times those who are popular or in cliques are the least happy! Find a good, true friend who will stick by you through everything!—Stephanie

Every school has cliques! There is almost no way around them! But that does not mean that you have to be a part of one or feel left out because you are not in one. Just find a nice group of friends who like you for you and not because you meet their criteria. But remember, if you are in a group of girls that you do not think is a clique, stand back for a second, examine it, and ask yourself, "How do we treat others?" and "Are we accepting others?" If you answered "Not good" and "No," maybe it is time to readjust your situation!—Emily

Last Word on Friends

Two are better than one because they have a good reward for their efforts. For if either falls, [her] companion can lift [her] up; but pity the one who falls without another to lift [her] up. Also, if two lie down together, they can keep warm; but how can one person alone keep warm? And if someone overpowers one person, two can resist him. A cord of three strands is not easily broken.—Ecclesiastes 4:9–12

Can You Relate?

1. Philippians 2:4 says, "Everyone should look out not only for his own interests, but also for the interests of others." What are some ways you can look out for the interests of others? Give examples.

2. Proverbs 4:23 says, "Guard your heart above all else, for it is the source of life." When it comes to boys, how can you "guard your heart"?

3. Proverbs 11:17 says, "A kind person benefits himself, but a cruel person brings himself trouble" (NET). How can this verse help you when it comes to mean girls?

4. Romans 12:15 says, "Rejoice with those who rejoice; weep with those who weep." What do you think this verse means?

5. Focusing on the blessings we have rather than thinking about the things we don't have can help cure our jealous thoughts. How can you become more content (happy) with what you already have and take the focus off of what you don't have?

6. Have you ever been left out? How did it make you feel? Do you think you've ever been guilty of leaving someone out? How might remembering this help you when you are the one being left out?

7. Have you ever had a best friend who ended up getting a new best friend? If so, describe how you felt.

8. What does God tell us about our one true best friend (Ephesians 1:4–5)?

FAMILY

5 Ideas for a Happier Home

by Pam Gibbs

Not too long ago, I woke up in the middle of the night and then couldn't go back to sleep. I decided to flip through the channels on my TV to see if I could find something boring to watch and fall back into a peaceful slumber (any news station will do the trick). Because it was so late at night (or early in the morning), there were a *lot* of infomercials on. As I looked at the titles, I noticed a pattern. All of them promised great results with little effort. "Five Steps to Tighter Abs." "20 Minutes a Day to Become a Millionaire." "$1,000 to Overnight Success."

What if I told you that you could do five simple things to make your home happier? Unlike the infomercials, these actions are based on Scripture. And following Scripture is always a good idea. These five ideas won't create the perfect home—it doesn't exist. But they can produce great results. Guaranteed.

1. Be last.

While He was on earth, Jesus told His disciples, "If anyone wants to be first, he must be last of all and servant of all" (Mark 9:35). Some of the arguments and unrest in your home take place because everyone is trying to be first. The first in the shower. The first to get the dessert. The first to grab the remote. What would happen if you chose to be last? Let your brother get dessert before you do. Rearrange your morning schedule so that you take the last shower but still have hot water. Don't worry about who gets to sit in the front seat. By following this simple rule, you'll stop countless fights before they even start.

2. Be humble.

Can I let you in on a little secret? You don't have to be right all the time. When I first got married, someone gave my husband and me a great piece of wis-

dom: You can either be right or you can be happy. A lot of arguments start because two people are trying to prove they are right. Sometimes, both of you can be right, so there's no sense in arguing. And sometimes you need to be humble enough to admit that you might just be wrong. Be willing to accept that your way isn't the *only* way.

3. Be helpful.

How much stress could you avoid in your home if you were helpful to the other people who lived there? If you drink the last bit of lemonade, make some more. If you use the last bit of toilet paper, take the time to get another roll for the bathroom. Help your little brother with his math homework. If you see empty dishes in the den, take them to the kitchen on the way to your room. What would it hurt if you were more helpful?

4. Be encouraging.

Living with a bunch of other people can get annoying. They can get on your nerves. Especially when your brother leaves his stinky soccer uniform on the bathroom floor. Rather than lash out and tell family members just how annoying they can be, try to be an encourager. Go to your brother's soccer game and cheer for him. Celebrate with your dad when he gets a promotion. Tell your mom she

What is your favorite way to have fun with your family?

Scan for Video Answers!

made great brownies for the lock-in. If telling your brother good luck is hard for you, write him a note instead. You can change the entire mood of your home by encouraging others.

5. Be responsible.

How many arguments have started in your house because your room wasn't clean? Or because your mom told you three times to load the dishwasher, and you still hadn't? How many times have you done your chores before being asked? One of the jobs for parents is teaching you to take responsibility for your actions. If you made a 60 on a test, admit you didn't study. Don't make excuses. Get the idea?

If these ideas overwhelm you, just try one or two at a time. Then pick up the others along the way. Before long, you'll notice a huge difference in your family. Guaranteed!

What the Bible Says About Family

"Honor your father and your mother, so that you may live long in the land the LORD your God is giving you."
—Exodus 20:12 NIV

A wise son brings joy to his father, but a foolish man despises his mother.—Proverbs 15:20

But if serving the LORD seems undesirable to you, then choose for yourselves this day whom you will serve, whether the gods your ancestors served beyond the Euphrates, or the gods of the Amorites, in whose land you are living. But as for me and my household, we will serve the LORD.—Joshua 24:15 NIV

Children, obey your parents in the Lord, for this is right. "Honor your father and mother"—which is the first commandment with a promise.—Ephesians 6:1-2 NIV

But from eternity to eternity the Lord's faithful love is toward those who fear Him, and His righteousness toward the grand-children of those who keep His covenant, who remember to observe His precepts. —Psalm 103:17-18

Listen, my son, to your father's instruction, and don't reject your mother's teaching, for they will be a garland of grace on your head and a gold chain around your neck.—Proverbs 1:8-9

Daddy Dearest:
Six Things Your Dad Would Tell You If He Could

by Pam Gibbs

When you were a little girl, you were the princess and your dad was the handsome prince. You dressed up in a pink dress, complete with the itchy tulle and frilly lace. Topped of with a crown and a scepter, you ruled the kingdom as your handsome prince was off fighting battles and protecting the kingdom from the wicked sorcerer.

Fast forward to present day. The crown and scepter have tarnished, and the lacy dress has been given away for another little girl to be a princess. You're all grown up now. The days of playing castle with your dad have been replaced by soccer matches and misunderstandings. Life is more complicated, even when it comes to your relationship with your dad. You know he loves you, but you just don't understand him. Why does he act weird when you and your friends talk about boys? Why does he keep telling you to "enjoy your childhood"?

Here are some truths your dad would tell you if he could:

1. "I'm not so good at words."

Science tells us that one of the ways guys and girls are different is in the way they communicate. Girls talk as a way of bonding. Guys talk to pass on information. In fact, guys don't really need to talk unless there is a purpose—a problem to solve or a decision to make.* Pay attention to the next time your dad talks to you: Is he helping you solve a problem? Is he helping you make a decision? Is he giving you information? Probably. He probably isn't going to explain how deeply he cares about you as you sit across from each other eating pizza. Not his style.

* http://www.washingtonpost.com/wp-dyn/content/article/2007/07/13/AR2007071301815.html

Tip for you: Text him and tell him you love him. He'll appreciate it. Then tell him in person too.

2. "I worry about providing for you."

God created men to be protectors and providers. Remember Adam and Eve? What was Adam's job? To work to provide for Eve and himself. Your dad works hard—not just because he's a perfectionist (he may be), and not just because he loves his job (he might). The biggest reason? He wants to provide for you. He wants to make sure that you have everything you need (not necessarily want!). A safe home to live in, clothes, food, a good college education—this is what motivates him to work hard.

Tip for you: When your dad comes home exhausted, don't immediately start asking for $20 to buy a new outfit or talk about how all your friends have phones except for you.

3. "I'm just trying to protect you."

Maybe you've heard the running joke about a dad cleaning his shotgun any time a guy comes over to see his daughter. Most dads wouldn't really do that, but I bet your dad will be watching very closely when you're old enough to have a boyfriend. He will ask questions. He will set boundaries. He's not trying to completely embarrass you; he's just trying to protect you. Remember the whole "protector and provider" thing? This is the protector role. He knows your heart and how easily it can be broken. He has seen what the outside world can do, and he would rather be battered and bruised himself than to see you hurting.

Tip for you: Go easy on your dad when you talk about having a crush or wanting a boyfriend. It's hard for him to imagine his little girl is old enough to like boys.

4. "I don't want you to miss any part of growing up."

Remember the days of princesses and castles and fighting the evil sorcerer? Those days were magic, and then poof! You became a tween. In a culture that constantly tells you to grow up, your dad doesn't want you to grow up too fast. There's too much you could miss along the way—bike rides with friends, sleepovers, the wonder of falling stars. He doesn't want you to grow up so fast that you miss the gifts that come with growing up.

Tip for you: Think of something that you and your dad did together when you were a child. Ask him to do that again. Play that board game. Go to that ice cream shop. Play that game of basketball in the driveway. It'll be good for both of you.

5. "It's hard for me to let you go."

Think of some of the best memories you have with your dad. Then ask your dad what his are. Chances are, some of those memories will overlap. Your dad has played an important role in your life. He helped you learn how to ride your bike; he wiped away the tears when you fell off. He stayed up past 2 a.m. to put together Christmas gifts for you and then watched you play with them the next morning. He helped you learn how to hit a softball and kick a soccer ball. He has invested his entire life into yours. That makes letting you go excruciatingly painful. When you start making decisions on your own and having opinions of your own, it's hard for your dad to let go. With every stride of independence you make, he's desperately praying that he taught you well.

Tip for you: Keep Dad in the loop as you make major decisions. You need his wisdom, and he needs to know you still need him.

6. "I miss our time together."

Does your dad ever start a question with, "Do you remember when . . ." and then launch into that same old story of when your family went on vacation and you got lost on the hiking trail and they had to send out a search party and . . . Why does he keep talking about that dumb vacation? Or last year's vacation? Or the time you went swimming when it was still too cold? Because he misses you. As you get older, your focus shifts from family to friends. That's normal. But that doesn't mean your dad likes it. He misses you.

Tip for you: Pull out an old photo album and look through it with your dad. Let him talk about what he remembers. Tell him what you remember too. That shared experience will stick in your memory banks, and that's a good thing.

One major way you can demonstrate love to your dad is to show him respect.

One more thing:

Your dad wants to be respected. That's a big deal for guys. Rolling your eyes at him is a huge sign of disrespect. So is ignoring him, slamming doors, and slumping your shoulders and walking away. One major way you can demonstrate love to your dad is to show him respect. Listen. Look him in the eye. Say "yes, sir." No, he's not perfect (neither are you!), but he's doing his best. And that deserves an extra dose of respect.

HELP!

When I was a little girl, my dad and I had a great relationship. We played games together. We went on hikes and rode bikes. We even wrestled, and I won sometimes! But now things seem really different. He doesn't come into my room as much. He doesn't hug me as often. And we never wrestle anymore. What's the deal?

Signed, Completely Lost

Dear Lost,

I know it seems like your dad is in another world, but *you* are the one in another world. It's called the tween years. And dads do not understand that world. You might as well be on planet Zork.

You're not a little girl anymore. You are going through a lot of changes inside and out. Your hormones are going haywire, parts of your body are developing in new and (sometimes) scary ways, and you are more independent. You are beginning to look more like a woman than a little girl. You have your own ideas and opinions. You are solving your own problems. And your mood swings are enough to give him whiplash. Where does a dad fit into this new world?

When you were little, he knew what he was supposed to do. He was the tea party guest, the boo-boo kisser, and firefly catcher. He was the monster-under-the-bed conqueror, knight in shining armor, and wrestling partner. But now . . .

What is his role?

Your dad is trying to figure out what this relationship with his little (grown) girl will be like. And he is trying to give you space. Things will feel weird and awkward for a while, but as you mature, you'll both discover that comfortable bond again. It will just look different.

In the meantime, help your dad out. Sit on the arm of his chair and lean in for a hug. Break out a game you used to play together. Put in a movie and huddle up to him on the couch. Those are unspoken reassurances that you still need your dad, and it will make him more comfortable about being a part of your new world.

Why Should I Obey My Parents?

by Pam Gibbs

"My parents are so lame."

"I can't believe my mom won't let me go to the concert."

"My dad is so protective. He won't let me do anything!"

Ever said those things to a friend? Chances are, you have. Most tweens have. That's because as you grow older, you want to exercise more freedom and make decisions on your own. Unfortunately, though, your parents don't always agree with your choices. They don't let you go to that party. Or that concert. They don't like your choice in friends . . . or crushes. When those moments come—when you and your parents disagree—you have a decision to make: do you obey your parents or do you defy them? Do you go behind their backs and risk getting caught? Do you lie in order to get what you want?

You may even ask yourself, *Why should I obey my parents?* Here are a few answers to that question.

Because Scripture tells you to obey your parents.

The Bible is very clear about how children are to relate to their parents. In both the Old Testament and the New Testament, God instructs His followers:

"Honor your father and your mother, so that you may live long in the land the LORD your God is giving you."—Exodus 20:12 NIV

Children, obey your parents in the Lord, for this is right.
—Ephesians 6:1 NIV

In the Old Testament, God was known as Father, and He commanded His people (the nation of Israel) to behave in certain ways. This is not because He wanted them to be miserable puppets. He didn't sit on the edge of the clouds ready to zap people with a lightning bolt whenever they disobeyed Him. What He commanded was rooted in His love for them. His commands were based on His wisdom and insight that were far beyond their ability to understand. And He is a model for your parents to follow.

God commands you to obey them because their rules and guidelines (commands) are rooted in love. Your parents set boundaries because they have wisdom and insight that you don't have. (Sorry about that, but it's true.)

Ultimately, obeying your parents is also obeying God. And that's reason enough to do what they say.

Because parents provide an umbrella of protection.

Have you ever been caught out in a nasty rainstorm? With wind whipping around and rain so heavy that you can't see across the street? I've been caught in one of those storms. I was walking with my boyfriend, and out of nowhere, the heavens opened up and the rain poured down in sheets so thick we could barely see the road. And we didn't have an umbrella. What happened? Duh, we got soaked, of course. Completely drenched. The "everything I am wearing needs to be wrung out a few times and put in the dryer" kind of wet. We. were. drenched. Hair dripping, water coming off the end of your nose, miserably wet. One thing could have prevented our misery—a simple umbrella. We probably would have still gotten our feet wet, but for the most part, we would have been dry and happy. "Singin' in the Rain" kind of happy.

Your parents' rules and decisions are an umbrella of protection over you. Stay under that umbrella and you will stay safe and secure. You'll still face hard times (like getting your feet wet under an umbrella), but you won't have to endure the consequences of disobeying them. How many teen drug overdoses could be avoided by following a parent's (and God's) instructions? How many car wrecks could be averted by not texting and driving? Get the point?

Because parents want you to feel secure and confident.

A story is told about a man who took a bunch of children out into a large, wide-open field with a bunch of toys—everything a toddler would want. Then he stepped back and watched what that those toddlers did next. Can you guess? They sat there. They wouldn't move. They wouldn't play with the toys. Next, the same man built a fence in that wide-open field, placed the same toys inside, and placed the same toddlers inside. Again, he stepped back and watched their reaction. Can you guess? Those same toddlers played and played and played and played. With every toy in that field. With each other. With the grass and flowers. Why? Because boundaries gave them confidence and security.

Boundaries give you an idea of what is expected of you. They also tell you what you are capable of doing. I wouldn't leave my daughter alone in the house when she was four years old because she wasn't capable of taking care of herself. She would be scared if I left her alone. When she gets old enough, I'll leave her there by herself because both she and I are confident that she can handle the situation. I just expanded her boundaries. As you grow older, hopefully your parents will expand your boundaries and give you more responsibility. They will allow you to do things at age thirteen that you didn't get to do when you were five. And they will expand those boundaries when you are fourteen and sixteen and older. Hopefully, when you graduate from high school, you will feel confident in your abilities because you have developed and tested them over time and under your parents' guidance.

Remember, your parents want the best for your life. Also remember that they aren't perfect. But they are doing the best they can under the leadership of God.

And that is the best place for *all* of you to stay.

Remember, your parents want the best for your life.

She Is SO Embarrassing:
When Your Mom Doesn't Act So Cool

by Vicki Courtney

When I was a teenager, my mom was designated as the taxi in charge of carting my friends and me on a trip to the mall. I was nervous the entire trip, wondering if she could make it the full five miles without embarrassing me (I seriously doubted it). As she pulled up in front of the mall, I breathed a huge sigh of relief. I was actually going to escape the car embarrassment-free!

Or so I thought.

As she was pulling up, a car in front of her slammed on the brakes, and my mom reacted by honking her horn loudly and screaming, "Great balls of fire!"

Fortunately, she didn't hit the car in front of her! My friends were hysterically laughing as we got out of the car, and for the rest of the day, they found any excuse to say, "Great balls of fire!" Arrrrgh! Like, what does that even mean?!

Although it was beyond mortifying at the time, I can laugh about it today. *Becoming* an embarrassing mom gives you a whole new perspective about your own embarrassing mom.

Not on Purpose

Moms don't set out to embarrass you on purpose. We may joke that our mission in life is to make your life miserable, but it's just a cover-up. The truth is, we just can't help it. We don't want to embarrass you. It just happens when we least expect it. The problem is that sometimes we are out of touch with your world. We don't get your funny jokes; we don't understand references to TV shows and movies. And your language? Totally foreign. We might as well be from Mars. But if you think about it, being out of touch with your world is probably a good thing. You don't really want that mom who dresses like you and your friends, talks like you and your friends, and wants to hang out with you and your friends. If given a choice, you probably want a mom who acts like a mom. Duh!

I realize that some of you have legitimate complaints about your mom's most embarrassing moments. I remember moms who would scream at their daughters in front of others, tease them about liking a certain guy, and criticize their daughter's outfits. Those problems go way beyond temporary embarrassment. That stuff needs to be addressed.

It's Okay to Speak Up

Some embarrassing moments happen because your mom just doesn't have a clue. But if your mom embarrasses you more often than not, sit down with her and calmly (!) tell her about the times she has embarrassed you. Most definitely talk about times when her words were hurtful. Most moms are reasonable people who can remember back to their own growing-up years when *they* had an embarrassing mom.

Leviticus 19:3 says, "Each of you is to respect his mother and father." Even when your mom makes your face turn ninety different shades of red, resist the temptation to lash out at her in front of your friends. Don't treat her with disrespect or make fun of her behind her back. Never yell at her in front of her friends. Instead, wait for the right time to talk with her (alone!) and let her know how her comments or actions made you feel. If you treat her with respect, she will likely treat you the same way.

Now, does this guarantee she'll stop parading around the house in those goofy brown loafers and white crew socks? Not a chance. You're stuck with that.

The good news is that in the future, you get to embarrass your own daughter. And you will. Trust me.

What's Your Most Embarrassing Moment?

When I got on stage and didn't know what to sing!—Anne, 11

Sneezing my gum out of my mouth in front of my crush!—Kaleigh, 10

Calling 911 on accident!—Danielle, 11

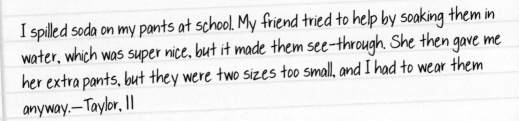

My pants ripped in school!—Kristie, 11

I fell over in my chair at school!—Alex, 10

I spilled soda on my pants at school. My friend tried to help by soaking them in water, which was super nice, but it made them see-through. She then gave me her extra pants, but they were two sizes too small, and I had to wear them anyway.—Taylor, 11

I called my young teacher "Grandma"—ugh!—Karly, 9

When I entered class and smiled with my new braces, and a boy said, "Ewww!" —Savannah, 12

I was at a softball game and said, "Get in your ready position, Huskies!" really loud. Then I realized that my team this year was the Wildcats! Oops!—Izzy, 8

A bird pooped on my head, and I never noticed it until someone at my party noticed.—Kaelan, 10

When I blew soda pop out my nose in front of six thirteen-year-olds! —Elizabeth, 10

I was talking to my friends while walking and ran into a wooden post. —Elise, 12

My crush found out I like him.—Mikaela, 10

One time, I got mixed up and called my teacher "Daddy"!—Allison, 10

Going to school and finding a pair of underwear in my pants! They had gotten stuck together in the dryer!—Keagan, 10

I thought someone else was my mom, and I hugged her.—Grace, 8

In third grade I tried to jump over a trash can in my classroom, and instead I fell in it.—Emma, 9

Quiz: How Close Are You and Your Dad?

by Pam Gibbs

How well do you get along with your dad? Take this quiz to find out! For each of the statements below, rate how true they are for you. The number 1 means the statement isn't true at all, any time, any place. Nope. Nada. Never. Then number 10 means the statement is true. Totally true. Nothing but true. At the end, you'll add up your score and see how things are going with your dad. Enjoy!

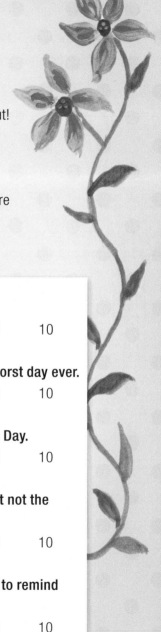

1. You like hanging out with your dad—just the two of you.

1   2   3   4   5   6   7   8   9   10

2. Your dad knows how to cheer you up when you've had the worst day ever.

1   2   3   4   5   6   7   8   9   10

3. You know exactly what you want to get your dad for Father's Day.

1   2   3   4   5   6   7   8   9   10

4. You don't like it when your dad has to go out of town. It's just not the same without him.

1   2   3   4   5   6   7   8   9   10

5. When you talk to your dad about your friends, you don't have to remind him over and over about who's who. He remembers.

1   2   3   4   5   6   7   8   9   10

6. Your science homework is so hard! Dad is the go-to guy for help with homework.

1   2   3   4   5   6   7   8   9   10

7. Your dad is at all of your softball games (or cheer competitions or . . .).

1   2   3   4   5   6   7   8   9   10

8. You would rather hang out with your dad than watch TV.

1   2   3   4   5   6   7   8   9   10

9. You know you are more important than your dad's job.

1   2   3   4   5   6   7   8   9   10

10. You like helping your dad with repair projects/yard work he does around the house.

1   2   3   4   5   6   7   8   9   10

Scoring:

0-33: Not So Close

From your answers, it looks like you and your dad are living in different worlds. However, that doesn't mean he doesn't care about you! Often, guys struggle more with being able to share how they really feel. Talking might not be their thing. Try to think of some ways to bridge the gap between the two of you. Ask him to help you with your next science project. Make his favorite dessert and sneak it into his lunch as a surprise. Watch him as he works on his favorite hobby. Ask questions about it. He'd love to explain it to you!

34-66: Sort of Close

Well, you may not tell him about your latest crush, but you have a fairly good relationship with your dad. Remember, you used to be his little girl, and now you're growing up way too fast! He may not know how to be a part of your changing world. You may need to make the effort to show him that you may be different, but you still love him a lot. Share with him something about your day, perhaps even a small dilemma you're facing. He may have some great advice, and you will help him know he's still important to you!

67-100: Way Close

Wow! You and your dad are best buds. Your answers indicate that the two of you get along great. You seem to enjoy hanging out with him, and he knows a lot about your world. And he makes the effort to show you he cares. Be sure to give him a gigantic hug and thank him for all he does for you and your family!

Note: Many girls today don't grow up with both their mom and dad living in the same house. Maybe your parents are divorced and your dad lives somewhere else. He might even live in another town, which makes it difficult to see him on a regular basis. Every situation is different, and it's still possible to have a closer relationship with your dad, but it may take some extra work. Consider video-chatting with him or touching base with him throughout the week by texting (or e-mail if you don't have a phone yet). With the technology options we have today, we are never really far away from someone..

It is also possible that your dad is no longer in the picture. Maybe he passed away, and you miss him terribly. (If that is the case, I am truly so very sorry for your loss.)

Or it is possible that you have a dad who just doesn't want to be a part of the family and doesn't make much (if any) effort to see you. (If so, I'm very sorry!) I want you to hear something: It is not your fault. Sometimes grown adults make very bad choices and behave in ways that God would not approve of. (And trust me, God would never want a dad to ignore his daughter or refuse to be a part of her life.)

If your dad is no longer in the picture, I want to offer you the hope that God is a Father to the fatherless. It even says that in the Bible!

A father to the fatherless, a defender of widows, is God in his holy dwelling.—Psalm 68:5 NIV

Also, there is this tender reminder for children who have parents who have chosen not to be a part of their lives:

Even if my father and mother abandon me, the LORD cares for me.—Psalm 27:10

From Lies to Wise: Word Scramble

by Susan Palacio

Look up the verses below and rewrite the lies back into wise Bible verses. Good luck!

Lie: A fool learns from his/her mistakes. (Proverbs 26:11)

Wise:_____

Lie: A wise man trusts in himself. (Proverbs 28:26)

Wise:_____

Lie: Gossiping is usually harmless fun. (Proverbs 26:22)

Wise:_____

Lie: Honorable girls love to be dishonest and tell lies. (Proverbs 29:27)

Wise:_____

Lie: A pretty face makes for a pretty heart. (Proverbs 27:19)

Wise:_____

Lie: Wealth lasts forever. Since you can take it with you when you die, spend your life chasing after it. (Proverbs 27:24)

Wise:_____

Lie: Learning to control your actions is foolish. If it feels good, do it! (Proverbs 29:11)

Wise:_____

5 Updates to Boost Your Relationship with Your Parents

by Vicki Courtney

Every app has updates. Version 1.3. Version 2.01. Version 3.2.4. You'll get notices on your tablet or phone telling you to update your app to the newest version. Why do developers continue to work on an app they've already sold? Because no app is perfect. You can always find areas that need improvement. Updates allow the app to work more smoothly, quickly, and effectively.

Your relationship with your parents is not perfect. And just like the apps, you can always find areas that need improvement. Try out the following "updates" to boost your relationship with your parents.

Update #1: Respect

Your parents deserve your respect. You may not always agree with their viewpoints or decisions, but you can always show respect. Don't roll your eyes or breathe a heavy sigh (you know!) when you don't want to listen. If you don't agree, don't be defensive. It only makes matters worse. Think about their side—their actions are rooted in love.

Rather than argue until you are all mad and frustrated at each other, accept your parents' decision and respect their rules and boundaries. And a simple "yes ma'am" or "no sir" can do wonders.

Update #2: Communication

"How was your day?" "Fine." "Do you have a lot of homework?" "No." "Are you ready for your science test tomorrow?" "Sort of." Is that really a conversation? I know it's hard when your parents start drilling you with questions, but look at the positive side: at least they care enough to ask! Try answering with more than one word. Believe it or not, their questions are not an attempt to annoy you—they just want to maintain a relationship with you. They care about what's going on in your life. Try sharing something small about your day, even if your parents don't initiate the conversation. You don't have to share your deepest secret. Just open up a little bit so they can peek inside your life. Trust me—a little communication goes a long way.

Update #3: Gratitude

Your parents do a lot for you. Braces, club teams, summer camp, driving on field trips, baking cookies for church, emergency runs to the store for poster board for your project. A parent's job is never done. Sometimes it's easy to take moms and dads for granted. A lot of kids around the world lack the essentials—a roof over their heads and three meals a day. Yet, most parents wear themselves out taking kids to countless activities, watching their games (even when its -4 degrees outside), and working extra hours so you can get that tablet or puppy for Christmas. Take some time to say thanks. E-mail your parents. Text them. And say "thanks!" when they go the extra mile.

Update #4: Grace

I know parents can be, well, embarrassing. Dad mows the lawn in dress socks, loafers, and shorts. Mom can't make it ten minutes without embarrassing you when you have a sleepover. And bless her heart, the waistband on her jeans comes up to her armpits. And she tucks her shirts in and wears a belt. Yikes! Most parents are not cool, so don't expect them to be. Remember, someday you will have kids who think you are uncool and laugh when they see your old pictures. And you might even want those mom jeans someday. For a costume, of course.

In the mean time, give them some grace. They *will* make mistakes. They *will* embarrass you. But they love you.

Update #5: Love

On my desk in my office sits an old, tattered sticky note I got from my daughter. It reads, "I love you very much." The ink is faded. I think I've spilled diet Dr Pepper on it a couple of times. You can't really read the word "very" because her handwriting was awful. She was only five or so when she made it. Taped to it is another note she "wrote." It says "I [picture of a heart] u moomy." Yes. Moomy.

Why do I keep those old notes? Because being a mom is a tough gig. I'll let you in on a secret: parents get worried, scared, frustrated, and discouraged too. Consider leaving your mom or dad a reminder they are loved—an "I love you" on a Post-it note, an e-mail, a text. It's guaranteed to make your mom cry—or at least put her in a better mood.

Honor your father and mother, which is the first commandment with a promise, so that it may go well with you and that you may have a long life in the land.
—Ephesians 6:2–3

Quiz: What Is Your Family's Personality?

by Pam Gibbs

If your family were a vehicle, which one would you be? Try out this quiz to discover which four-wheeled form of transportation would best represent your family.

1. When the phone rings, what happens?

a. What phone? We each have our own smart phone!

b. You all grab it before anyone else can.

c. You're not home to hear it.

d. You wait to hear the message and call back when you have more time.

2. The perfect Saturday afternoon with the family would mean:

a. Going to see the new Egyptian exhibit.

b. Inviting your friends over for supper.

c. Playing video games together.

d. Checking out the new computer store.

3. Which would your family most like to do together?

a. Listen to music in the park

b. Help at the church

c. Go bowling

d. Create a new app or watch a documentary

4. When it comes to cleaning house:

a. Where's the maid?

b. We'll work together to get it done.

c. What chores?

d. Spic and span is the motto.

5. If your dad got a huge bonus at work, how would you spend it?

a. Go on a trip

b. Buy an outdoor firepit

c. Buy something fun for your game room

d. Save it for college

6. Which of the following stores would your family most likely go to:

a. The Apple Store! You can never have too many electronic toys!

b. Anywhere with lots of people! We don't mind a crowd. The more, the merrier.

c. A store that sells outdoor/adventure gear

d. A bookstore

7. If you all showed up late to church, what would your family do?

a. Try to sneak in without being noticed

b. Apologize to the pastor afterward

c. Make a joke about it

d. What are you talking about? We're NEVER late!

8. Vacation time means:

a. Manis, pedis, and massages all around (well, at least the girls in the fam).

b. Sharing a condo on the beach with other families.

c. Amusement parks, water parks, rafting trips, laser tag

d. Relaxing at the park with a picnic or doing a home improvement project.

9. If you were stuck in a cabin for the weekend, what would you miss the most as a family?

a. Internet access

b. Soft drinks

c. Video games

d. Books

10. If your family were a piece of literature, what would it be?

a. A classic, like Shakespeare

b. A cookbook

c. A mystery-thriller

d. A biography

Mostly A's—A limo

You appreciate the best life has to offer. You like to pamper yourselves and enjoy culture around you—music, museums, libraries, concerts. You would rather stay in a nice hotel than go camping anytime. Sometimes you are so focused on yourselves that you don't notice hurting people around you, so be careful.

Mostly B's—A party bus

Your family would organize a block party and offer to cook all the burgers. Your family loves to interact with others. You might even offer a room to a teen in trouble or a college kid who can't go home for Christmas. Be careful, though, being around other people all the time can be draining, so take time to be alone as a family too.

Mostly C's—An RV

When it comes to adventure, your family will try almost anything. You don't like sitting at home in front of the TV. You'd rather be out experiencing life and exploring the world around you. On the flip side, it's hard for you to be serious and practical. Sometimes the dishes just need to be washed.

Mostly D's—A car that's practical and paid for!

Your family is smart, practical, and disciplined. You might even be a bunch of overachievers. You love to push each other to achieve more, but you can also be too competitive with each other. And sometimes your family has a hard time relaxing. It's okay not to do extra credit. Try something fun together instead.

Being a Good Sister

by Whitney Prosperi

When I was five years old, my younger brother and I were playing in the new house being built for my family. To save money, my mom and dad were doing a lot of the painting themselves. My brother and I were playing in one of the rooms they had just painted the whitest white you have ever seen. Like white-as-snow white. White-piece-of-paper white. The walls looked perfect, and Mom and Dad told us not to touch the walls—or even go near them.

The walls stayed that beautiful color—until the orange soda. I promise it was an accident. Those cans always explode and spew out fountains of soda when you don't want them to—like when you're near a newly painted white wall. I simply popped the top, and an atomic bomb of orange exploded all over the perfect, white walls. What do you think we did? Run to tell our parents immediately? Of course not. We panicked. We ran into another room and played there. We acted like nothing happened and avoided that room altogether.

Later that night, when my parents saw the walls, they asked my brother what happened. He told them I was responsible for the eruption on the walls. Then they asked me. And I wimped out—and blamed my brother. Because I was the oldest, my parents believed I was telling the truth, and they punished my little brother. I don't think my little brother remembers because he was too young when it happened, but I remember. I still feel sad when I think about it.

You probably have your own story—a time when you got your brother in trouble, ruined your sister's shirt, or blamed your younger siblings for the mess in the garage. It's easy to do. Siblings are around all. the. time. And sometimes, they can drive. you. crazy. Maybe your younger brother constantly follows you around, wanting to hang out with you when your friends are over (how lame!). Or your sister might not take good care of your stuff, the stuff you worked hard to earn. Sometimes being respectful and kind and loving toward your siblings is the last thing you want to do. Siblings often lash out at each other and say hurtful and mean things to each other when emotions run high and patience runs low.

We all know the children's rhyme that says, "Sticks and stones can break my bones, but words will never hurt me." Although that little saying is easy to remember, it really isn't true. The sting from words can last longer and cut deeper than any rock. And girls seem especially keen at knowing just the thing to say that will hurt the worst.

What kinds of words fly out of your mouth when you're talking to your brothers and sisters? Do you regularly tell them they are stupid? Do you scream at them when they bug you? Do you make fun of them? Or just plain ignore them? Keep in mind that your brothers and sisters will remember the things you said to them—the good and the bad. Colossians 4:6 says, "Your speech should always be gracious, seasoned with salt, so that you may know how you should answer each person." You have the opportunity to build up your siblings—or tear them down.

Fill in the blank. My siblings are easy to get along with. All I have to do is _____.

Scan for Video Answers!

God put you and your siblings in your family for a reason. He wants you to be a positive influence on them. You can do this by choosing kind words and forgiving them when they bug you. You can listen to them when they have a bad day or include them in your more grown-up activities. The more you choose to show respect and kindness toward them, you'll discover that they don't bug you so much. In fact, you may realize that the whole reason they kept pestering you was because they just wanted your attention.

Your speech should always be gracious, seasoned with salt, so that you may know how you should answer each person.
—Colossians 4:6

10 FUN THINGS TO DO WITH SIBLINGS

1. Put together a scrapbook of family photos and mementos.

2. Watch an old movie together.

3. Make homemade ice cream.

4. Read a good book together. C.S. Lewis's *The Chronicles of Narnia* is a great series.

5. Work on a jigsaw puzzle together.

6. Catch fireflies together.

7. Play "Would You Rather?" by making up questions to ask each other. (Would you rather eat a mouth full of dirt or a mouth full of worms?)

8. Build a Lego fort.

9. Show your younger siblings how to make the perfect paper airplane.

10. Build a fort in your house using blankets and other materials.

Goodbye, Hello:
What To Do When a Parent Remarries

by Pam Gibbs

Your mom and dad already messed up your world by getting a divorce. You had to adjust to the new living situation, the visitation, the juggling of schedules, the name changes, the new address (for at least one parent), and the new reality of life with divorced parents. It was weird not seeing your parents together anymore. Seeing them at football games but sitting separately. Having only one of them come home from work. Talking and texting and video chats with one while living with the other. Then things take another turn when your parents start dating other people. Now that's just weird. You know it's perfectly normal for them to move on with their lives. But still . . . weird.

And now, just when life seemed to settle into a new "norm," a bombshell:

One of your parents is getting remarried.

Um, who's in charge of this roller coaster called life? Could we just slow it down for a while?

Life on a Roller Coaster

Unfortunately, life does feel like a roller coaster sometimes. And unfortunately, you can't just ask the operator to let you off at the next go-around because the ride feels out of control. Life keeps moving forward, and you must adjust constantly to what comes at you along the way. Fortunately, you're not the first person to adjust to life with a stepparent and new stepfamily. Others have gone through the same experiences, so you aren't alone. Here are a few things they would say to you if they could sit down with you over a latte:

Your stepparent isn't trying to replace your biological one. No one can take the place of your parents. You have a unique relationship with each of them. Your new stepparent knows this, so he or she isn't trying to make you forget your parents. When he (or she) asks questions, offers to help, and joins in at events, he (or she) is trying to develop a relationship with you. If the idea of having another parent just wigs you out, think of the new adult in your life as a mentor. He or she is older and has lived through experiences different than those of your parents. They will offer their wisdom and perspective, but the idea is *not* to replace your biological parents.

You want your parents to be content and not lonely, don't you? Remarrying is a way for your parents to create new lives for themselves. This does not mean they don't care about you or your life. It just means that your parents need people with whom they can share their lives. Just like you want to find and marry that special someone someday, so do your parents. They want to experience that just as much as you do.

Respect is a must.

You don't have to instantly love your new family member(s), but you do need to respect them. You may not like your parent's new spouse. You may not get along with her. You may not like to be around him. She may get on your very last nerve with her goofy, high-pitched laugh. He may tell the corniest jokes or dress like he belongs in the '70s. You don't have to spend the day together joking and making memories that will last forever (cue sappy music). But you do need to respect your new stepparent. Scripture tells us to give respect to others (Romans 13:7). That means you don't get to call them bad names or treat them badly. You don't get to try to get between your parent and new stepparent to try to drive them apart. It means treating them like you would treat other adults in your life.

Learn the new rules.

A blended family has its own set of rules. And those rules will develop over time. That means your blended family (new stepparent and any stepchildren) will need to talk—a lot. Who is responsible for doing the dishes? Will your new stepparent discipline you? Does your stepparent have the authority to give the thumbs up or thumbs down when you want to do something? How will holidays work? What traditions do you celebrate with them? When you have a question, ask it. There's no good reason to keep it to yourself. Other people in your family may be asking it too.

Accept the situation.

It is what it is. If you take things as they are and not the way you want them to be, adjusting to this new life will be much easier. You can't un-marry your parent and new stepparent. It's a done deal. You can't change the fact that new people are in your life: new siblings, cousins, grandparents, and aunts and uncles. Will you be close to all of them? Who knows. But they won't magically disappear because you wish your life could go back to the way it was before.

Give your stepparent a chance.

You may discover that he or she is actually pretty cool. He makes your mom smile, and you haven't seen that in a long time. He knows how to fix stuff around the house and knows as much about horses as you do (and that's a lot). Or maybe your dad's new wife played the same sport you do. She can play electric guitar or is a pro at board games. And she's a *much* better cook than your dad. The truth is, having a stepparent can actually be a good thing in your life, not make it worse.

Don't Wig Out:
Loving Older Family Members

by Susie Davis

With a roll of my eyes, I grabbed my car keys off the kitchen counter and walked toward the garage. My mother had given me the job of driving my grandmother to the local beauty center to buy a new wig. My grandma had just moved in with our family because she was going through chemotherapy treatments for cancer. The chemo had caused her hair to fall out, and she wore wigs to cover her bald scalp.

I certainly didn't know why *I* should have to run this errand with my grandma when my mom could do it. Besides, didn't my mom care that I had made plans with my friends? Didn't she know that I was loaded with homework? Didn't she know that a sixteen-year-old, busy with high-school activities, just didn't have time to drive her grandmother all the way across town to look at wigs?

As we got in the car, I quickly turned up my music, hoping at least to enjoy the trip, and just as quickly my grandma started asking me about school.

"How is high school going for you, sweetie?"

"Fine," I replied.

"Do you like your classes?"

"Yes," I mumbled.

"Are you still dating that nice boy?"

"Uh-huh," I stammered.

With the conversation going nowhere fast, she quietly hummed and looked out the window.

By the time we arrived at the beauty center, I was hoping for some quick decision-making on her part. If she decided on a wig quickly, I could meet up with my friends without being late. But my grandmother took her time, looking at this wig and that, asking what I thought about the style and color. I was growing more and more impatient every minute.

Finally, a sales woman came over to help her make a decision. After trying on several, she carefully fitted my grandmother in the wig of her choice. My grandmother was happy, and I was relieved.

As we started the trip home, I decided that speeding things up a little in the car would get us there sooner. I noticed my grandmother tightening her grip on the seat as I sped along. Finally, when she could no longer stand it, she asked me to slow down, and just as I was about to explain to her that I wasn't driving that fast, I took a corner too sharply and ran into a tree.

I got out of the car, checked the bumper, and was relieved that there was no damage to the tree or the car. I got back in, apologized to my grandma, and drove carefully home.

That whole scene shook me up. The thing that bothered me most was the fact that I was so impatient. So selfish. So uncaring. My schedule and my fun mattered more than everything else in my life—including my grandmother.

The Bible has some things to say about honoring people who are older or elderly. Leviticus 19:32 says, "You are to rise in the presence of the elderly and honor the old." To honor someone is to respect her, and you show that respect through your actions. When we give someone respect, that means we are interested in pleasing her and placing her needs before our own. In my situation, I was dishonoring my grandmother, and I was dishonoring God.

Some years later, my grandma did eventually die of cancer. I'll never forget the phone call I got while I was away at college. My dad called late one night to tell me she had slipped into a coma, which is kind of like being so sick that you are asleep and you can't be awakened. The doctor said that she wouldn't live much longer. I borrowed a friend's car and quickly headed home, crying all the while.

When I arrived at the hospital, I walked in to see my grandma. There she was, unable to say anything. I tenderly touched her hand and called her name. I stood looking at her and remembered my time with her—the times we had laughed while playing a card game called "Pig," and the times we had enjoyed watching her favorite shows together. I also remembered the arguments with her and the times I had been impatient and selfish.

Then I silently prayed that God would forgive my ugly moments with my grandma. I prayed that He would forgive my impatience and my lack of concern. I prayed that she would know I loved her. And then, through tears, I spoke to her.

"Grandma, I love you. I am so sad that you are in so much pain. Thank you for being such a great grandma. I also want you to know how sorry I am for not honoring you in all the ways I should. Please forgive me. Please let me know that you forgive me and you love me."

In the very next moment, her eyes fluttered, and I felt her fingers lightly lift and touch my hand. I leaned forward and hugged her weary body as gently as I could. She had spoken in the only way she could, letting me know that she forgave me and that she loved me.

Sometimes it is hard to remember to honor the elderly people in your life. When I was young, I didn't always do it right, but maybe you can learn from my mistakes. Think of ways to honor those people by putting their needs in front of your own. Whether it is doing little errands for them or listening to their stories, find some time to care for them in a way that will show you love them. You'll be honoring them—and you'll be honoring God.

You are to rise in the presence of the elderly and honor the old.
—Leviticus 19:32

Hair Gel, Elmo Hands, and Ostrich Poo:
Moms Can Have a Bad Day Too

by Pam Gibbs

My day started off badly when my "always wants to be at school earlier than the other kids" daughter had a major meltdown because nothing looked good on her. (I know you can relate.) Nothing puts a mom in a cranky mood like her nine-year-old screaming at the top of her lungs that I didn't care about her and that I was the meanest mommy in the world for making her go to school with uncool clothes.

On the way home from dropping her off at school, I took off the ball cap I had worn. I took one look at my hair, and I reached *that* point—that point when you feel like the ugliest girl on the planet because you have the worst hair *ever*. (You've been there, I know.) I had to get a haircut. Now. I was desperate. I got dressed quickly and headed for the quick clip shop in the strip mall before a much-needed lunch with a friend.

The aforementioned fast-cut place did a fair job on my hair, but apparently they don't do styling early in the morning. The stylist didn't even dry it. (Who knew you actually had to *ask* to have your hair dried?) I let it air dry while running errands. One of those errands turned into a stop at Walgreens for some hair gel so I didn't look like a *total* dweeb while eating lunch with my friend, which was in just a bit. If I hurried, I could finish all of my errands.

Unfortunately, in the middle of Walgreens, my thrifty gene kicked in and I chose a travel-size gel I'd never used before. I trusted it because it was the same brand as the one I usually bought. But . . . it was a different formula. Like the difference between Elmer's glue and Super Glue different kind of formula. I put a little into the palm of my hand and tried to work it through my fingers like

I usually do with hair gel. Only my fingers don't move. The gel has melded my hands to each other. So I'm sitting in my car with my hands plastered together with goop that only a jackhammer or blow torch could separate. I can't go home and I wouldn't dare go back in the store and ask for the bathroom key with my hands stuck together like I'm about to bow my head in prayer. I decide to wipe off the layers of goop onto the closest victim in my car: my favorite jacket. Unfortunately, that jacket is crimson red fuzzy. Yeah, you know where this is going.

Now my hands are covered with goo *and* the fuzz from my jacket. My hands resemble Elmo's. I look around the car and see my water bottle. That water must be sacrificed so I can fix the problem, lest my hands draw the attention of every three-year-old in the tri-state area. Ten minutes later and an entire bottle wasted, I can at least feel my skin enough to take off the rest of the hair gel by using an entire bottle of hand sanitizer. I now have the cleanest hands in the metro area. Okay, my morning has been shot, but maybe I can manage a little work before my lunch date. I get out of the car and circle around to the passenger's side to grab my laptop for a little writing. Then I see it.

Apparently, ostriches can now fly. Because a herd or flock or gaggle of them has apparently made its way to my house. And apparently, these birds ate something that disagreed with their finicky stomachs. The amount of ostrich poo plastered on the passenger's side of the car was astounding. Impressive. And absolutely gag-inducing.

I am supposed to pick up my friend for lunch, but I would *never* subject her to the sight and smell—never mind the feel—of the ostrich poo because it's all over the car door handle. So, I have to stop at a car wash, where I spend twenty minutes trying to power-wash the poo from my car. I think it must be the same consistency of the hair gel. I'm sure my friend will buy me lunch for this sacrifice of time.

If you've ever seen anyone power-wash poo from a car at close range, then you know what happened. Yep, blow back. I finally got the ostrich poo off, but now the right side of my body is soaking wet and smells like a cross between dish detergent and car wax. I hate to be cold and wet, so the next stop was the nearby McDonald's, where, by the way, I saw Elvis selling newspapers (only in Tennessee!).

I commandeered the hand dryer in the bathroom for roughly four hours (or so it seemed) until my clothes didn't feel like I'd been through a car wash. I must have looked impressive, holding out the side of my shirt and slapping it against my skin so it would dry.

I had just enough time to make my lunch appointment. And I'm stressed beyond words. And it's only 10:45 a.m.

Why am I writing about the worst morning in American history? To show you a glimpse into the day of an ordinary mom. While you're at school, we are at work. Or running errands. Or volunteering at the church. And in the course of that day, anything can happen. We get stressed and frustrated. We get overwhelmed and angry. We get insecure and make poor decisions (like a haircut at a strip mall). We face our own set of tests, mean girls, and competitions. They just look a little different than yours.

The next time your mom comes home and looks like she has been running a marathon at a sprint, give her a moment to relax and decompress from a difficult day. Don't overwhelm her with requests and demands. Don't ask her what's for dinner. And don't whine about your horrible day because you had to wait ten minutes for the bus.

Sometimes your mom needs a break too.

This Ain't the Brady Bunch:
Tips for Getting Along with Stepfamily

by Pam Gibbs

The *Brady Bunch* was a blended family. A widow and a widower got married and moved into the same house with all six of their children. And they all got along and solved all of their conflicts in thirty minutes or less.

Talk about un-reality TV.

Getting along with a stepfamily doesn't happen overnight, and the problems aren't solved with a quick talk over dinner and a hug. There are no rules to go by when two stepsisters play on opposite basketball teams. Or when two stepbrothers have both dated the same girl. Nobody has the perfect formula for working out conflicts over fall breaks, religious beliefs, or birthdays that overlap. There is no Brady Bunch solution for those issues. Learning how to adjust to new family members is a process, a learn-as-you-go experience. You may not have a choice about your family situation, but you do have a choice in how you treat your new (and old) family—for better or worse.

Be patient.

Be patient with yourself. And your biological parents. And your stepparent. And your new stepsiblings. Give yourself and everybody else space and grace to adjust, figure out emotions, make mistakes, and learn along the way. Unrealistic expectations will only add to the stress of this new family situation. Just like your parents' relationship developed over time, these new relationships will develop over time. It won't happen overnight.

Talk about everything.

Nobody can read your mind, so pouting, sulking, giving others the silent treatment, and being quietly resentful won't do anybody any good—especially yourself. Talk about how you feel. Ask questions. Give your opinion. Tell others what you want and need. Ask about how your families will juggle Christmas break. Find out if your new stepparent will have the authority to dole out discipline. Talk about who is responsible for what around the house. Simply asking stepsisters and brothers when they prefer to take their showers and adjusting accordingly can make a huge difference.

Find a pro to talk to.

You are new to this whole stepfamily thing, but lots of people are pros—they've been through it before and know what it's like. Find someone outside of your family who has been where you are now. Ask her how she adjusted. Find out what she would do differently if she had to do it all over again. Talk to her about what drives you nuts, what scares you, and what you're worried about. Having been through this, she will give you insight that no one else can. And she will remind you that you are loved, even though you may not feel it sometimes.

Talk to God.

I know that sounds like a churchy answer, but praying *does* help. Knowing that the God of the universe is listening even when your family is in chaos can bring you peace. He knows your situation and your new family members. He created them too, remember? Ask Him to guide your new family. Ask Him to give you patience and grace and wisdom (see tip #1). Pray for the willingness

to change the things that annoy your family. He cares about your situation and wants to help if you will let Him.

Give the new family members a chance.

You may hate the situation. You may think this re-marriage is the worst idea ever. You may have concluded that this whole blended family thing will end in a disaster of epic proportions. And you could be completely wrong. This blended family could turn out to be one of the biggest blessings in your life. You may discover that your new stepdad is really cool and that having a younger stepsister is actually a lot of fun. You'll never learn that if you don't give this new family a chance. You couldn't stop the union. And you can't stop this new family from existing, so go into it with a positive attitude (as much as you can). Be open to doing new things—different foods, a new store, a different church. You might just find that you actually like this new family.

Then you will be blessed twice over—with two families that love you.

Even Tweens Can Be Role Models!

by Whitney Prosperi

Do you remember being in the third grade? You probably idolized the fourth and fifth graders. You wanted to talk like, dress like, look like and act like the girls who seemed soooo much more mature, confident, and independent. And when you moved to the fourth grade, you idolized the middle-school girls. Whether or not you realize it, you're always looking for role models in your life. In fact, you could probably name three or four you have watched and wanted to be and act like.

But here's a question: Have you ever thought of yourself as a role model?

If you have a younger sister, brother, or even a cousin or two, you are an example. Whether you like it or not. And even if you don't have any younger relatives, you can bet *someone* is watching you. It may be a neighbor or girl at your church. It could be the younger sister of a friend. It could even be a girl in a younger grade than yours. She wants to act just like you. She listens as you talk to your friends and notices the choices you make.

Today's culture encourages tweens to grow up—as fast as possible. Dress like the models. Go to Rated-R movies. Like guys who are waaay older than you. Cuss like the teenagers who ride your bus to school. However, God's perspective on your life is very different. First Timothy 4:12 urges us, "Let no one despise your youth; instead, you should be an example to the believers in speech, in conduct, in love, in faith, in purity." God wants you to be an example to others even though you are young. Rather than waste your influence, why not use it? Consider the possibility that *your* example may change someone else's life or influence a whole nation. You. just. never. know.

Think back over the last forty-eight hours. If someone were watching you, what kind of example did you set? Were you mean or critical? Did you pass along a juicy piece of gossip? Think about your actions. If a parent or youth leader were to grade your behavior, would you be happy with that grade? Have you shown love to others, even though they are different than you? Have you forgiven people—even in your own family? This may be the hardest place of all to set an example. If you have younger brothers and sisters, your patience may be pushed to the limit. It's much easier to act mean, get back at them, and make them as mad as they've made you. But think about what might happen if you were kind and gracious and forgiving. What you do and what you say matters.

A friend of mine became a Christian when she was about ten years old. She tells the story of how she constantly left Bible verses in her little sister's room and told her about Jesus every day. She taught her songs and Bible stories so that her little sister would understand how to follow Jesus. And one day she had the opportunity to pray with her sister as she committed her life to Christ. Instead of being irritated and frustrated with her sister's immaturity and aggravating quirks, she chose the role of encourager and model—and her sister has been changed.

Will you provide a good example for the girls who are younger than you? If you don't want a younger girl to use foul language, then make sure you don't. If you want your younger brother to be nice to your friends, then you have to show him how. Guard the messages you put in your mind through TV, movies, music, and the Internet, and you'll be sending a message to those who look up to you.

Do you take seriously the role God has given you in your family? In your school? On your team? You can be a role model in a thousand places every day. If you haven't thought about how you could influence others, stop right now and say a prayer asking Him to help you as you set a Christlike example for others to follow.

Will you set a positive example in the choices you make? In your speech? In your faith? In how you love others? You may not believe it, but younger girls watch everything you do, and they will copy you someday. Make sure that as they are following you, you are following Jesus.

Younger girls watch everything you do, and they will copy you someday.

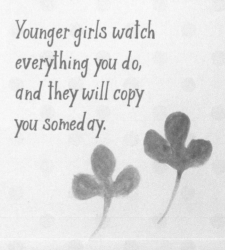

Moving Out, Moving On:
When Your Relationship with Your Siblings Changes

by Pam Gibbs

I am the youngest of three children. My brother and I are ten years apart, and my sister and I are six years apart. (If you want to do to the math for practice, go ahead, but my brother and sister are four years apart. Now back to the story....)

When I was fairly little—like four or five—my siblings and I got along great (or as well as you could in a house with one bathroom). We went swimming at the local pool during the summer. We had watermelon-seed-spitting contests off the front porch. We endured family reunions by swimming together at the lake. One of my fondest memories involves the three of us watching *Star Trek* together (you can stop snickering now). We had a ginormous crimson pillow, about four feet long and three feet wide. My brother would lay down with his head on the pillow and stretch out his arms. The two of us sisters would snuggle on either side of him with our heads in the crook of his armpit. He wrapped his arms around us (tickling us from time to time), and we watched the show.

As my brother and sister got older, things got . . . weird. My brother moved off to college when I was just eight, and he only came home at Thanksgiving and Christmas. He was a lousy letter writer, and we didn't have texting, social media, or live video chats. When he came home, things were different. Even though he was "home," he didn't stay at home. He wanted to hang out with his high-school buddies or go to the football game (I grew up in Texas where football is everything). He didn't want to sit in front of the TV and watch *Star Trek* with his immature sisters.

About the same time, my sister turned boy crazy. Instead of listening to records with me (small discs made of vinyl that played music at different speeds . . . Google it), she would talk on the phone for hours with her friends—about guys. Who liked whom. Who had the coolest haircut. Who got asked out to homecoming. She turned in her Barbie dolls for roller skates and her teddy bear for a tennis racquet—because *that guy* played tennis.

My world was off-center. What had happened to my brother and sister?

They were growing up.

I was growing up too, but I didn't notice it because my brother and sister were changing at such a rapid pace (which is normal, by the way). All I knew was that my two favorite playmates were gone off to college and gone goo-goo for guys.

Perhaps you can relate, especially if you are the younger sibling. Your brother and sister used to love being with you—making a fort out of blankets and furniture, racing bikes down the street to see who was the fastest, even watching movies together. But now, your interests are changing. Things just aren't the same. That's okay. Life is all about constantly growing and changing and hopefully maturing. What do you do when your siblings change? Here are just a few ideas.

Use technology to your advantage.

Fortunately, you can keep in touch with your siblings in lots of different ways. If you already have a cell phone, you can text them. You can set up video chats so the two of you can catch up. You can message on social media sites (with your parents' permission, of course).

Make a pact.

To help bring you closer together, agree that you'll snap a photo of each other at least once a week, showing what you've been up to. This will give you a glimpse into your siblings' lives, and you can all see how you are changing physically.

Use postcards.

Ask your mom or dad to buy you and your siblings postcards and stamps so you can send quick notes to each other just to say hello and I love you. When you or your siblings travel, you can pick up postcards from the locations and send them. It's fun to get cards from all over, and they mean a lot coming from siblings. And since sending a letter or postcard is so uncommon nowadays, it'll be fun to get a note in the mail!

Make a reservation.

If you know one of your siblings is coming home for the weekend, ask for some alone time. Don't request a whole day—you will be disappointed. Ask to go get some coffee or ice cream together. Or watch old home movies of when you were all little. Asking beforehand will increase the likelihood of one-on-one time. This same tip applies if you have a sibling at home but you never see her.

Be patient.

Your siblings aren't trying to leave you out. They haven't forgotten you. They are not purposely trying to make you sad. They are changing, just like you are. And change is difficult. Be patient with them and with yourself. The relationship will find its new normal, and you'll learn how to feel comfortable with each other again.

One major thing to keep in mind: your sibling misses you too. Just because your sister moved out or your brother got super busy doesn't mean they don't get sad. They miss the times you hung out. They feel the awkwardness of the changing relationship and want things to get better. They still care about you very much.

They love you. That's the one thing that doesn't change—even if their address does.

The Pros and Cons of Being an Only Child
by Vicki Courtney

No fighting over the cinnamon roll with the most icing. It's yours. Want to claim an extra bedroom in the house to store your bazillion toys and stuffed animals? Go for it. No arguing over which movie to watch on family movie night. You win. No sharing the bathroom with a sister who hogs the mirror and leaves the lid off the toothpaste. It's all yours. No need to call "shotgun" when racing to the car to claim the coveted passenger seat. Go for it. And every Christmas morning, all those presents sitting under the tree? They are all yours!

There are many perks when it comes to being an only child. Ask any of your friends who are growing up with pestering brothers or annoying sisters, and chances are, they've had moments when they wish they could trade places with you and get a taste of your one-and-only world.

Likewise, I imagine there are also times when you've wished for siblings. Life always looks more attractive from a distance. Sometimes the grass looks greener at your friend's house—you know, the one with four brothers and sisters. Or the sky looks bluer at your cousin's house—the one where the volume is always set on high and chaos is common.

There are pros and cons to being an only child. In those times when you are feeling a need for a little sibling company, ask your parents if they can arrange some cousin-time or allow a friend to tag along on a weekend road trip. Maybe they'd even be open to allowing you to take a friend along on a family vacation or letting you go stay with a friend or family member who has a house full of kids for a few days during the summer break. Don't assume your parents can read your mind and automatically know when you are in need of a little company. Being an only child can be a real blessing. Recognize the benefits, but learn to speak up when you are feeling a little lonely.

Last Word on Family

If you have no desire to worship the LORD, choose today whom you will worship, whether it be the gods whom your ancestors worshiped beyond the Euphrates, or the gods of the Amorites in whose land you are living. But I and my family will worship the LORD!
—Joshua 24:15 NET

Can You Relate?

1. Read Ephesians 6:1. Why should children obey their parents?

2. Why do you think your parents give you rules? Is it to be mean and make your life difficult or to protect you and make your life better?

3. When was the last time you said "thank you" to your parents for something they did for you . . . or just because? What can you thank your parents for this week?

4. What is something little you can do to remind your parents that you love them?

5. Colossians 4:6 says, "Your speech should always be gracious, seasoned with salt, so that you may know how you should answer each person." How can this verse help you in how you respond to your parents and siblings?

6. Read Leviticus 19:32. Why do you think the Bible tell us to "honor the old"? Share some examples of how you can honor your older family members (grandparents, etc.).

7. Name three people who are role models in your life.

8. First Timothy 4:12 says, "Let no one despise your youth; instead, you should be an example to the believers in speech, in conduct, in love, in faith, in purity." What are some ways your can show God's love to younger girls who are watching and listening to you?

The WORLD
Around Me

Can You Use Technology Too Much?

by Pam Gibbs

You are a technology native.

Huh?

That term simply means that technology has always been a part of your life. You have never known a time in history (or even in your home) without computers, a GPS, tablets, cell phones, laptops, and smart TVs. You can speak emoji and LOL and BRB and TTYL as easily as you can speak English.

Being in a world of technology has its benefits. You can access information 24/7. You can find out anything you want, any time. You can talk to a friend who lives on another continent. You can text your mom to let her know why you're late (if you're old enough to have a phone). You can research about a charity in Ireland that saves endangered animals and tap into its live webcam feed. The world is at your fingertips—literally.

Can you ever have too much technology?

Yes.

The New Addiction—Technology

Here's the problem with technology. Rather than you controlling it, it can actually control your behavior. I'm not talking about artificial intelligence or robots taking over the world or implants in your brain connecting you to some supercomputer buried deep in the earth.

I'm talking about addiction.

According to Merriam-Webster, Mr. Dictionary himself, addiction is "a strong and harmful need to regularly have something (such as a drug) or do something (such as gamble)."*

Addiction to technology means that you feel the constant urge to be on your phone or on your tablet or to use some other electronic gadget. You feel lost without it. You constantly use it, even when you are doing something else.

Sound like you?

*http://www.merriam-webster.com/dictionary/addiction

Here are a few questions that will help you see signs of addiction to technology:

- Have you ever lied to your parents so you could have more screen time (time with phone, gaming, tablet, etc.)?

- Do you regularly use technology when you wake up or before you go to bed?

- Has your schoolwork ever suffered because you spent too much time texting, looking at social media, playing games on your tablet, or using other apps?

- Have your parents ever had to take away your phone or tablet or ground you from the computer?

- Have you ever lied (even to yourself) about how much you use technology?

- Does using your phone or your tablet interfere with sleeping or eating?

- Does the thought of being away from technology make you nervous or anxious?

- Have you ever felt defensive or ashamed about the time you spend with technology?

How do you make sure technology— such as your phone, computer, TV, or video games—doesn't become more important to you than your real world and your relationships with friends, family, and God?

Scan for Video Answers!

Busted? Me too.

What's the harm, though? Seriously, what's so wrong with texting your friends or playing games. Nothing—until it begins to take over your life. When technology takes all of your time, you have a problem. When you spend all of your money on apps or games, you have a problem. When other people feel like you care about your phone more than you care about them, then things have gotten out of control.

Is Getting Rid of Technology the Answer?

Obviously, you cannot avoid technology altogether. Technology is a part of your life. However, it doesn't have to *control* your life. You can take some steps to make sure that *using* technology doesn't turn into *abusing* it.

113

Try these ideas:

Don't take your device into the bathroom.

Seriously? You can't be away from your gadget long enough to take a potty break? Think about it from a health perspective: now you've got those nasty bathroom germs all over your device. You can't wash those off in the sink. Eww!

Put your device away at meals.

There's no need to text, watch videos, play games, send pictures, or mess with apps while you are eating, especially when you are eating with friends and family. That's just rude.

Turn off devices while watching TV.

Your attention is divided. If you want to be on your digital device, turn off the excess noise (the TV). I know, I know, you can do both. But doing both at the same time takes away the enjoyment of both. You can't really get into a movie or show if you're constantly texting or playing a game. Whatever you are doing, give it your undivided attention.

Set hours.

If you have your device with you all day long, every single day, you may have a problem. If you use your phone to wake you up in the morning, ask your parents to buy you an alarm clock. If you explain why, they'll fork over the money on the spot.

Turn off alert signals.

This will keep you from jumping to your device every time you hear it beep, ding, sing, or honk. Who wants to be a slave to the sound of birds chirping? It will also help you stay focused on whatever you are doing at the moment.

Use real words and your real voice.

If your best friend is sad about something, don't text her. Go to her house or call her. Let her talk as long as she needs. Send your grandmother a real birthday card instead of posting a note on social media. Walk into the other room and tell your dad thank you instead of texting him.

One last thought:

When you spend all your time with someone or something and have no room for God, that's called idolatry. And that's a problem. *Nothing* is more important than your relationship with God. He deserves the first place in your life, not your cell phone, your social media updates, or a game level you're trying to beat.

Cell Phone Do's and Don'ts

by Vicki Courtney

You may not have a cell phone just yet, but when your parents do allow you to have one, here are some general rules you'll need to remember:

Turn off your phone at church. Don't just put it on vibrate, or you'll be tempted to answer texts you get from your friends.

Put the phone on vibrate when you are at a restaurant. It's rude to read texts or play on your phone when you're eating with friends or family members.

Don't text when you're in the movies. You may think you're not bothering anyone, but the bright light is annoying to people around you.

Don't broadcast your life to others by talking loudly on the phone. Nobody wants to know what you had for dinner or who you have a crush on. If you need to talk with someone, go somewhere private, away from lines or large groups of people.

Don't text when you're angry. If you're ticked off, cool off and then call the person. (I know, it's weird to actually talk on the phone.) Some feelings just don't come across right in a text.

Don't text something you'll regret. Remember, once you text it, it's out there. It can be passed along to anyone, anywhere. You can never get it back.

Don't abbreviate too much. Stick to the symbols and terms most people know. This especially applies to adults—especially your grandparents. They may be cool enough to text, but they probably don't understand WRUD (what are you doing?). Besides, if you make up an abbreviation, some-one might misunderstand you. That's how fights start with friends.

Don't be insensitive or rude. Don't ever use texting to hurt someone's feelings or to bully others. Not only is that in-appropriate and mean, it's against the law. You could get in serious trouble.

Quiz: Are You a Hothead?

by Susan Palacio

Have your parents ever told you, "Stop overreacting! It's not that big of a deal"? I bet that didn't help you cool off in that moment, did it? Like it or not, your parents are probably right. When it comes to anger, it's easy to overreact to the situation or the person. How do you react when you face tough situations or difficult people? Take this quiz to find out!

1. It's time to visit your grandparents, so your family piles into the SUV for the two-hour trek. About thirty minutes into the trip, your little brother starts to kick the back of your seat. You tell him to stop, but he just kicks your seat harder and harder. You . . .

A) yell, "Stop it!" and then stop yourself and ask him nicely to please stop.

B) scream at the top of your lungs, "Stop it, or you'll be sorry!"

C) ask him to stop, and when he doesn't, you ask for your mom's help.

2. In English class, you take a test you really weren't ready for and don't feel good about the results. When your mom asks you about your test, you . . .

A) tell her it went okay, but there were some questions that didn't seem fair.

B) tell her the test was really hard and that you should have spent more time studying for it.

C) cross your arms and launch into a long explanation of how unfair the teacher is and how no one likes her.

3. Your sister "borrows" your headphones and takes them to the pool. When she returns them, they reek of sweat. You . . .

A) march directly to her room, throw your head phones on the bed, and say, "*You* messed them up! Now *you* have to buy me a new pair!!"

B) ask your sister to please not take your headphones without asking.

C) let her know how frustrated you are, and tell her to use her own headphones next time.

4. You're a star softball player, and your team has made it to the semifinals during a weekend tournament. You're in the last inning, and the umpire calls a strike that was totally a ball. His call causes the batter to walk and the other team to score. You . . .

A) shout, "What!???" Then you kick the dirt and gripe to your teammates before pulling it together for the next play.

B) yell to your team, "It's okay, guys. Let's get the next one. We can still win this!"

C) throw your glove to the ground, throw your hands in the air, and scream at the umpire, "You need some glasses! I can't believe this! This is so unfair!"

5. Mom says you can't spend the night with Madelyn because you have to be up early for dance class the next morning. You . . .

A) are disappointed but hold your tongue and try to make other plans with Madelyn.

B) roll your eyes, stomp to your room, and slam the door behind you.

C) sigh and say "fine" in a frustrated, disrespectful tone. Later, you go back and apologize to your mom.

6. Everyone is talking in class, but the teacher calls you out. You are the only one to get punished and have to write an extra report for class. You . . .

A) snap, "But Mrs. Cole, everyone is talking. Why am I the only one who got punished?" Later, you regret losing your cool and go back and apologize.

B) realize you were wrong for talking, even though no one else got punished. You write your report and turn it in the next day.

C) bark, "What? That's so unfair!" All afternoon, you talk about how mean and unfair your teacher is.

7. You and your friend, Lindsay, agree to visit the coolest amusement park together over the summer. You both promised to go with each other, but Lindsay got a free ticket to go with her church. You find out that she was planning to go with them and wasn't planning to tell you about it. The next time you see her, you . . .

A) ask why she didn't tell you. You explain that your feelings were hurt, and ask her if she still plans to go with you too.

B) frown at her and say sarcastically, "Thanks a lot, Lindsay. Some friend *you* are!"

C) burst out with, "Lindsay, why are going without me?? You totally ruined every-thing!!! My summer is wrecked because of you! I can't believe you'd do that!"

8. To be funny, your friend Sophie texted an embarrassing picture of you to your entire group of friends without asking your permission. You . . .

A) reply to the entire group and tell an embarrassing story about Sophie, adding in a few extra things she told you in secret.

B) reply to the group, mentioning what happened, and telling Sophie she was really rude to send the text to everyone.

C) reply privately to Sophie and tell her that you wish she had asked your permission first before sending the picture.

Total your score by using points in this legend:

1. A-2; B-3; C-1
2. A-1; B-2; C-3
3. A-3; B-1; C-2
4. A-2; B-1; C-3
5. A-1; B-3; C-2
6. A-2; B-1; C-3
7. A-1; B-2; C-3
8. A-3; B-2; C-1

How did you score?

Calm, Cool, and Collected!

If you scored between 8 and 11, congratulations! You handle "heated" situations with a lot of "cool"! You realize that even though you may be frustrated, reacting with calm is always the best choice. You try to calm yourself down by counting to ten or waiting a few minutes to respond. Keep up the good work!

Frustrated but Focused!

If you scored between 12 and 16, you tend to overreact initially, but you usually calm down before things get out of hand. You still need to work on your gut reactions, which is hard to do. Remember, a gentle answer turns away wrath, so make sure you've dealt with your own anger before speaking or doing anything—even if you need to go to another room for a moment to calm down.

Sizzlin' Hothead!

If you scored between 17 and 24, you are a hothead! You let your anger get the best of you, and it shows! You don't hold back your anger, but let it out, no matter who you hurt in the process. Instead of showing self-control, you usually look foolish by overreacting. Practice counting to ten if you're angry, or remove yourself from the situation until you can calm down. Keeping your anger in check requires self-control, but the good news is that self-control just happens to be one of the fruits of the Spirit (Galatians 5:22–23)! Pray and ask God to help you develop more self-control.

Say What?
Positive vs. Negative Words

by Vicki Courtney

I love speaking at mother/daughter events across the country. I especially love getting to meet all the girls and their mothers. At one event where I was a speaker, a lot of moms came up to meet me. They had such kind things to say about how God spoke to their hearts through what I had said and how it encouraged them.

Until I met one woman at the end of the line.

She had *nothing* kind to say. Instead, she began listing her complaints one by one. I stood there for what seemed like forever and tried to be as patient as possible as she went on and on about the sanctuary being too cold, the bookstore being out of small T-shirts, and even how the sandwich at lunch didn't have enough lettuce on it. Seriously! I didn't control the temperature in the sanctuary, the T-shirt sizes, or the lettuce on the sandwiches.

Finally I couldn't take it any longer, and I gently interrupted and said, "I'm just curious, but was there *anything* positive that God may have shown you?" She just stammered and stuttered while she tried to think of something. Finally she said, "Well, I just thought you should know what was wrong, so you can work to make it better."

Um, okay. I think it's helpful to know when something needs improvement, but I wondered why this woman couldn't have shared a couple of positive things along with her complaints? Or shared her complaints in a more pleasant tone? Yikes!

Here's what's crazy: months after the event ended, I could still remember this *one* woman's complaints, but I couldn't recall all the encouraging comments the other women had made. What's up with that?

I bet you're the same way. It's hard to forget when someone makes a mean, nasty comment even if it's stuck in the middle of a pack of nice ones. Several verses in the book of Proverbs remind us that our words can be "life-giving water" that can "satisfy the soul" and "nourish life." I hope my words encourage and refresh others, like a cool drink on a hot day.

And trust me, when I get a thank-you card or e-mail from someone who has kind words to say, I save it for a rainy day. You never know when a meanie will come along!

The words of a man's mouth are deep waters,
a flowing river, a fountain of wisdom.—Proverbs 18:4

A fool's mouth is his devastation, and his lips
are a trap for his life.—Proverbs 18:7

From the fruit of his mouth a man's stomach is satisfied;
he is filled with the product of his lips.—Proverbs 18:20

Life and death are in the power of the tongue,
and those who love it will eat its fruit.—Proverbs 18:21

Activity: Cheap Talk or Sweet Talk

by Susan Palacio

What do your words say about you? Finish this story to find out if you're a sweet talker or cheap talker!

Being in the _____ (grade you're in) grade isn't easy. Especially

with _____ (a girl's name), who is the meanest girl in

_____ (grade you're in) grade. She's a real "MG" (Mean Girl).

   You and your BFF, _____ (name of one of your BFFs),

are both trying out for the advanced _____ (type of dance)

class. The teacher only accepts _____ (number between 10 and 20) students

in a semester. You and _____ (same name of one of your BFFs)

have both dreamed about making the class for _____ (number from 1 to 12)

months and already talked about practicing after school every day together.

_____ (name of MG) is a _____

(synonym for really good) dancer, but she is not a nice person! At the tryouts,

she even teases you about your _____ (body part), saying

it's gross and _____ (adjective like "gross"). A few days

later, the afternoon the teacher posts the results, you, _____

(same name of one of your BFFs), and _____ (name of

MG) all show up at the same time!

You see it! There's your name, _____ (order like 1st, 2nd, etc.) on the list! You quickly scan the list and do not find either _____'s (same name of BFF) or _____'s (name of MG) name. Neither girl made the class. Disappointed, you turn to _____ (same name as BFF) and say, "_____

_____"

(something nice you would say to make her feel better).

Then, you see _____ (name of MG) out of the corner of your eye. This is your chance to get her back for all the nasty things she said about you. You realize it's wrong, but surely she deserves it. You finally decide to say: "_____

_____"

(something to make her feel better or something to get revenge for her mean words).

What did you say to MG?

If you treated MG the same way that you treated your BFF, then you're a sweet talker! You can hold your tongue when tempted to say something hurtful, even when it seems like the perfect time to get revenge! No matter what the situation, you realize that your words have power and it's always best to be kind, even if someone's not kind to you.

If you got revenge and rubbed it in MG's face that she didn't make the class, then you're a cheap talker! You took the opportunity to hurt her with your words like she hurt you. Now you're both hurt. Even though it's tempting, getting back at someone for her harsh words isn't the wisest response. And it doesn't honor Jesus. Hold your tongue until you can use it to build up others instead of tearing them down.

The Gold Medal That Wasn't:
A Story About Listening

by Vicki Courtney

When I was in middle school, I joined the track team. I was pretty fast in the short- distance races and would generally place in the top three and get a ribbon. I'm not sure if you still get a ribbon for track, but I always enjoyed tacking my first-place ribbon on my bulletin board at home. I had a great coach who liked me and encouraged me to be a runner.

One day at practice, my coach announced I would be running in a long-distance, half-mile race at the up-coming track meet. I had never run such a long distance before, but I felt pretty sure I could do it. I had two weeks to get into shape, and my coach took the time to give me some good training tips.

One bit of advice my coach gave me was to resist the urge to run fast in the first lap. She told me to find a good medium pace and save my energy for when I needed it in the final lap. She had me

practice with some of the other girls who ran long distances, and I kept up with them on the first lap. On the second and final lap, I was usually behind, but I was beginning to get used to the distance and finished somewhere in the middle of the pack.

The day of the track meet arrived, and when they announced the half-mile race, I lined up with the rest of the runners in the starting blocks. It's always nerve-racking when you're waiting for the familiar, "Runners to your mark . . . get set . . . go!" When the gun went off, signaling the start of the race, I left the blocks at full-speed. I don't know what happened, but I kept up my fast pace, even though I was going against the training and advice of my coach. Being ahead of the pack felt good, and I thought I could keep up the pace and win. I wanted another blue ribbon for my bulletin board.

You probably know what happened. By the second lap, I was beginning to lose energy as the other girls were gaining on me. By the time I stumbled awkwardly across the finish line, I was miles behind the other girls, bent over with a cramp in my side and a look of embarrassment on my face. I came in dead last. No ribbon for my bulletin board.

I'll never forget the coach's look of disappointment when I walked over to her after the race. All she said was, "Vicki, you discovered why it's important to listen to your coach when you're training for a race. I bet you won't make that mistake again." And you can bet I didn't.

The next time my coach put me in a long-distance race, I followed her instructions completely. I finished somewhere in the middle of the pack, but I didn't care. Anything was better than coming in dead last and having everyone in the stands stare at me with a look of pity!

Proverbs 13:13 says, "The one who has contempt for instruction will pay the penalty, but the one who respects a command will be rewarded." Take a minute and thank God for the advice He gives through His Word. Also thank Him or sending others to give you good advice. Ask Him to help you put aside your pride the next time someone gives you good advice—and follow it. You'll be glad you did, with or without a medal.

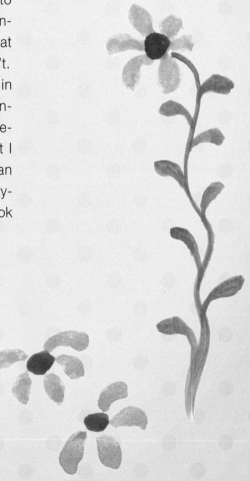

The one who despises instruction will pay the penalty, but whoever esteems instruction will be rewarded.

—Proverbs 13:13 NET

Quiz: Are You Rude?

by Vicki Courtney

The Bible tells us to "Show proper respect to everyone, love the family of believers, fear God" (1 Peter 2:17 NIV). Do you show respect for the people around you, or are you rude and disrespectful? Take this quiz to find out! (Check your answers on the following page.)

1. You walk into a store with your friends just as an elderly woman is walking out. You . . .

A) hold the door open for her and wait for her to walk through first.

B) let her get the door herself. You're in a hurry!

2. Your mother calls to you from another room. You can't hear her clearly so you . . .

A) come closer and call back, "Ma'am?"

B) scream back, "I can't hear you! What do you want?!"

3. Your grandmother calls you to wish you happy birthday. She asks you a bunch of questions about your day. You . . .

A) tell her about your day and thank her for the birthday money she sent you.

B) answer "yeah" to all her questions. You can't wait to get off the phone!

4. You and a friend are sitting together in church. Your pastor preaches a little longer than normal, and you begin to squirm. You . . .

A) try very hard to concentrate on what he is saying.

B) start texting your friends or playing hangman on the church program with your BFF. It's just too hard to concentrate.

5. Your mom makes cinnamon rolls one morning for breakfast. You and your sister (or brother) rush to the table. You spot the one you want— the most ooey-gooey roll on the plate. You . . .

A) let your sister (or brother) choose first.

B) grab it fast. The icing isn't as good if it gets cold.

Total up your answers. How many A's did you have?

If you have 5 A's:

You are a polite, respectful young lady. Keep up the good work!

If you have 3 to 4 A's:

You have some room for improvement, but you're off to a good start!

If you have 1 to 2 A's:

Girl, you need to do a manners check! Chances are, you can be rude, disrespectful, and impolite. Ask God for help in showing more respect. You'll discover that others will show you respect too.

The Monster Inside Me

by Pam Gibbs

Like most girls my age, I was afraid of monsters. I was convinced one lived in my closet. He had plenty of room to hide with all the junk I stashed in there. One night, I went to bed before everyone else. I was the youngest, so that was the rule. In a few minutes, I was nestled under the covers, surrounded by my favorite stuffed animals as usual. That's when it happened. A long, hairy arm reached out from under the bed and grabbed the edge of my nightgown. In one fluid motion, I screamed, yanked at my nightgown, and jumped up onto the center of by bed. My parents rushed in and turned on the lights. Out from under my bed came my big brother (ten years older), laughing so hard he couldn't catch his breath.

He wasn't laughing later when my parents grounded him for life (or so it seemed).

The Real Scary Thing

You and I both know that monsters don't live under your bed or in your closet. But did you know that we all have a little monster living with us? She won't show up at night to take you away to her magical lair. She won't snatch you away when your parents go to sleep. She doesn't always come out, but she's there. Her name?

Me-Monster.

Have you met her? She thinks of herself first and really hates sharing—especially those brand-new markers with the perfect tips! Sometimes she takes the bigger half of the cookie and gives her little sister the smaller one. And every now and then, she pouts and gives Dad the silent treatment if she doesn't get her way.

Everyone has a me-monster in them. She is sneaky, scary, and selfish. And she can show up when you least expect it. You can be hanging with your friends, having a great time, and out of nowhere, she pops out. You can be babysitting your brother, walking in the mall, or watching a movie. No place is safe from her reach.

And when she appears with a roar, it is not a pretty sight. People around her usually don't like to see her. She's rude. And mean. The most awful thing about her is a selfish heart.

How the Me-Monster Was Born

Even Mom and Dad have me-monsters. Adam and Eve committed the first sins in the Garden of Eden, and everyone born after them (which is everyone in the world) was born with a sin nature. That means we were all born with a tendency to think about ourselves all the time, and it takes a lot of effort to think about others.

We like to put our wants and desires above others' needs. It's a "monster" of a problem!

How to Tame the Me-Monster

We need help dealing with this problem, and God has given us the weapon to fight off this monster. It's found in Matthew 22:37–39 (NIV):

"Jesus replied: 'Love the Lord your God with all your heart and with all your soul and with all your mind.' This is the first and greatest commandment. And the second is like it: 'Love your neighbor as yourself.'"

I'm sure you've heard these verses before, but did you know that *neighbor* doesn't just mean the neighbors in your neighborhood, but *everyone*? Notice that it says before we can love our neighbor as ourselves, we must first love God with all our heart, soul, and mind. That means we love God completely, more than anything else.

Here's the good news: God knew that the me-monster would be a problem for us, so He gave us His strength and Holy Spirit to help us defeat her. We certainly couldn't do it alone. Ask God to help you make unselfish choices. Once you start doing that regularly, it becomes easier to do!

As extra encouragement, God has given us examples in the Bible to follow. Here are a few people who relied on God's strength to act unselfishly:

- Daniel told King Nebuchadnezzar to keep the gifts that were supposed to be given to him (see Daniel 5:17).

- Abraham gave Lot first pick on his new homeland (see Genesis 13:9).

- Jonah asked to be thrown into the sea because he knew he was causing the storm that was endangering other people in the boat with him (see Jonah 1:12–13).

- Joseph stuck by Mary when she was pregnant with Jesus when he could have divorced her (see Matthew 1:19–24).

- The Christians in the New Testament shared their money, possessions, and homes with others (see Acts 4:34–35).

The next time you are tempted to unleash the me-monster, remember that God gives you the strength to control her. You may not ever get rid of her, but you can learn to tame her.

Attitude Check

by *Susie Davis*

Did you know that you can say a *lot* without using words? Without using your mouth? You can tell how you feel about a situation using nonverbal communication. Nonverbal basically means "without words." Communication means "getting information to someone else." When you are getting information to someone else without your words, you are communicating nonverbally. Confused? Keep reading.

Imagine being outside playing soccer with your neighborhood friends. You just scored a goal, and your team has taken the lead. Then your mom steps out on your front porch and calls out, "It's time to come inside and start on your homework." You look up and yell back, "Just one more minute, Mom. We're in the middle of a game!" Your mom shakes her head and replies, "No, come inside now—it's time for homework."

You look up, make a sad face, and say, "But Mom, please . . . " She straightens her back, puts her hands on her hips, and gives you "the look."

You know you are two seconds from being in big trouble. You roll your eyes, heave a heavy sigh, toss the ball to your friends, and slouch your way up to your front porch. Then when you get to the front door, you give your eyes one final roll and give one more deep sigh, your shoulders dipped low. Your mom looks you square in the face and says, "You'd better watch that attitude, little lady, or you're gonna get yourself into trouble. "

As you headed inside, you didn't need to utter a word to your mom or your friends to communicate how you felt about leaving the game and starting on homework. The eye-rolling, the sad face, the heavy sigh, the slouchy walk, and the drooping shoulders said to your mom (and everyone else!), "I'm angry about coming inside, and I want you to know about it!" Your mom also said some things nonverbally when she shook her head, straightened her back, and put her hands on her hips. Those actions said, "I am serious about you obeying me and getting in the house to do homework."

Have you ever heard the saying that actions speak louder than words? In the story above, your actions spoke volumes, but you didn't need to use a single word. Nonverbal communication is very powerful. Scientists who study nonverbal communication say that people will believe what they see your body saying instead of the words coming out of your mouth.

Try this experiment: Look in a mirror, smile, and say, "So nice to meet you." Say it again, but this time, make a face that looks bored. Next say it with a face that shows happiness. Then fear. That's a funny experiment, but you have to admit that the words get lost when you see a face that sends a different message. The truth is, people are more likely to believe your face than your words.

God made you to speak with your words and your bodies, and it's a wonderful thing to be able to do both. But you need to remember you are responsible for both. When your body language shows a bad attitude, you are responsible for what message you are sending, just like you are responsible for the words you say.

When you have a bad attitude and you're griping and complaining nonverbally—usually because you are not getting your way—that nonverbal communication ends up getting you in trouble with your parents, your teachers, or even your friends. When they see you roll your eyes or sneer or make a face, you are saying something unkind with your body. And because nonverbal communication is the first thing people "read" on you, it is the thing others will believe.

Philippians 2:5 says that our attitude should be the same as that of Christ Jesus. Think about that for a minute. Would Jesus roll His eyes at His mom? Do you think He would say unkind, ungrateful things nonverbally? Sometimes responding the way Jesus would is really hard, but God can help you with your attitude! Start praying that God changes your attitude and what your body language says to others. The next time you feel that nasty, bad attitude creeping in, just whisper a prayer: "God, let me have the same attitude as Jesus." Very soon you'll be saying "so long" to that bad attitude!

Your attitude should be the same as that of Christ Jesus.

How to Fight Fair

by Pam Gibbs

You won't always agree with other people. You and your friends will argue. You and your parents will disagree. And you and your brother (or sister) will most likely yell at each other at some point. But did you know that fighting with people is normal? Not the knock-down-drag-out fist fight you see in the movies, but the "I can't believe you took all the hot water in the shower *again*" kind of argument.

Most of the time, you argue because you think your needs and wants are being ignored. You need hot water. You want a new cell phone. And sometimes you argue because of miscommunication. You thought your bestie started a rumor about you (she didn't). Or your parents said no, and you thought they said yes.

How the fight started isn't nearly as important as how you finish it. Did you know there are rules? Think of arguments like a boxing match. In boxing, you can't hit someone below the waist. You can't tackle. You can't pull hair. In the same way, there are good rules to follow for fighting fair when you disagree with someone. (And no, you cannot pull your sister's hair under any circumstance!) Here are some important tips to follow if you want a good outcome to your fight.

Take five.

No, I'm not referring to a kind of candy bar or a boy band. "Take five" means take a few minutes (at least five) to cool off. When you are really, really angry about something, you will probably say things you'll later regret. Rather than yelling at the top of your lungs (which won't help), go to another room for a few minutes. Take some deep breaths. Try to calm down the thoughts racing through your head. When you can talk in a normal tone of voice, go back and try to talk (not yell!) about what happened or what you disagreed about.

Don't hit below the belt.

That's an actual rule in boxing. You're not allowed to hit a person below the waist—for obvious reasons! Doing so can cause permanent damage. The same rule applies for a verbal fight. In this case, hitting below the belt means saying something to intentionally hurt someone just because you want to hurt her (or him). Don't call someone else names—especially ones that you know will get you grounded. Don't threaten to share secrets or threaten to stop loving the person. Some things just aren't cool to say, even if you are ticked.

Don't attack.

In boxing, you can't just run at your opponent and tackle him to the ground. In an argument or fight, you can't just attack the person either. Attacking sounds like this: "You are so mean!" or "You just don't care about me!" or "You make me so mad!" These kinds of statements feel like you are attacking a person's character. Instead, try to begin the sentence with the word *I*. "I feel hurt when you tell me I'm not old enough. . . ." or "I feel hurt when you hang out with so-and-so and leave me out."

Don't start the silent treatment.

Seriously, do you think this will make the situation any better? You'll only get more angry and frustrated because the other person doesn't understand what's going on, and your friend (or family member) will get frustrated because you won't talk about it. Can I give you a hint? The other person likely has *no* idea why you've started the silent treatment. If he or she knew, then you would have talked about it by now. And if you start the quiet game in the middle of the argument, then the problem doesn't get resolved and everybody ends up frustrated. The silent treatment is a sign of immaturity, so ditch it.

Keep the finish line in sight.

What do you want to happen? Do you want to keep being angry? Do you want to stay frustrated? Or do you want a solution instead? The goal is to work through a problem, not to make yourself (or someone else) miserable. If what you are doing doesn't help fix the problem, change what you are doing!

Be very clear.

Decide what you want first. Then say that. "I would like you to stop telling rumors about me." Or "I would like you to shorten your shower by five minutes so I can have hot water too." Or "I would like you to ask me before you use my markers." See how different that is from yelling? You're more likely to get what you want by saying it.

Ditch two words: never and always.

These two words are often used in fights, but they are misleading. Your parents don't always

135

say no. Your mom never lets you stay out late? The words *always* and *never* make the other person out to be the bad guy. And nobody likes feeling that way.

Listen.

Your parents may have a good reason for saying no, but if you immediately start yelling about how horrible your life is (is it, really??) or how mean they are, you won't ever learn the reason for their answer. And you'll look immature too.

Stick to one topic at a time.

You can't start off complaining about how none of your friends have to do chores and then jump to how they never punish your brother for bugging you when your friends are around. When you add topics, it's trying to watch two TV shows at once. Everyone involved will get confused and frustrated, and nothing gets solved.

Don't stay mad. Learn to let it go.

Once the fight is over, give yourself some time, but then let go of your anger. Letting anger simmer will eventually lead to someone getting hurt. And sometimes it will be you. You won't always get what you want when you have an argument. Part of growing up is learning

that you don't always have to have your way. Demanding your way all the time is for bratty five-year-olds. You're older and better than that.

In the New Testament, Paul said, "Do not let the sun go down while you are still angry" (Ephesians 4:26 NIV). Obviously, Paul wasn't telling you to try to stop the sun from setting. He was saying, "Don't go to bed angry." Now, you can't always solve a conflict immediately. But you *can* talk it out quickly, before bitterness and resentment kick in. The sooner you work through the problem, the sooner you can be on better terms again. And that's a win-win for everyone.

Do not let the sun go down while you are still angry.
—Ephesians 4:26 NIV

A Card, Gymnastics, and a Bunch of Stickers
A Lesson in Taking Revenge

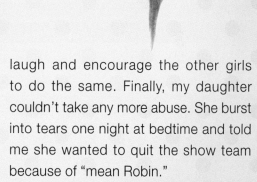

by Vicki Courtney

When my daughter, Paige, was seven years old, she took a gymnastics class that met several times a week. Some of the girls in the class who mastered the more difficult skills were chosen to perform on a show team. After watching that team perform, my daughter was determined to be a part of that team. She worked diligently to master the skills, and her work paid off. She was asked to be a part of the team.

Her first weeks of practice on the show team were pretty rough. She was the new kid, and the other girls would often leave her out. One girl in particular was especially mean. She teased Paige when Paige would try a new trick; she would point and laugh at Paige when she tumbled down the mat. Sometimes this girl would cut in front of Paige and

laugh and encourage the other girls to do the same. Finally, my daughter couldn't take any more abuse. She burst into tears one night at bedtime and told me she wanted to quit the show team because of "mean Robin."

I wanted to call Robin's mom so badly. I wanted to call the cheer coach. I decided to pray with Paige first and see if we couldn't solve the problem by following God's Word. I shared with Paige that Matthew 5:44 says, "But I tell you, Love your enemies and pray for those who persecute you" (NIV). If you look up the word *persecute*, you would find a definition that says, "to annoy or trouble persistently." We decided that we would pray for Robin. After we prayed, Paige said shockingly, "Mom! I know! I can make a card for Robin!"

The next day Paige gathered her craft supplies and went to work making a card for Robin. She even tucked inside some stickers she had just gotten for her birthday. The next day, we headed to practice with the card in hand. We got to practice a little early so Paige could give the card to Robin before class started. When Robin walked through the door, I prayed a silent prayer for my daughter as she walked over and gave Robin the card.

Slowly, Robin opened the card, read the sweet message, and looked at the stickers. I could hardly believe what happened next: a smile broke out across her face, and she hugged Paige! After that, Robin was much nicer to Paige. They didn't become best friends, but peace prevailed in practice.

I can't promise that making a card for your enemy will bring the same results, but I can promise you this: If you pray for the people who persecute (annoy, bother, pick on, etc.) you, and if you give the matter to God instead of taking revenge yourself, you will certainly bring a smile to God's face.

"But I tell you, Love your enemies and pray for those who persecute you."
—Matthew 5:44 NIV

Wise Words: Starting Middle School

In some cities, fifth and sixth graders are in middle school instead of elementary school. If you're in middle school (or about to be), check out this great advice from older girls who were asked the question, "What one piece of advice would you give a girl going into middle school?"

Don't just stick to one group of friends. Get out there and meet people. You'll regret not meeting a lot of people.—Sarah

When I went to middle school, the freedom I had was a little too much. I was saying some bad words and probably not making the best choices. It wasn't until a year or so ago when I really knew I was being stupid. Never forget about God, because He never forgets about you.—Leah

Be yourself; if you want people to like you and be your friend for who you are, you can't act all the time!—Maria

Be organized and prepared! See if you can find a couple of friends who are in your classes, and together you can avoid getting lost! You can also pray! God is always there!—Jennifer

There are so many pressures in middle school to do things that will get you accepted, but those things are not always healthy and are usually not the things that God delights in. Guard your heart and your mind by reading the Bible, and don't be afraid to call out to God when being set apart for Him seems too much to bear.—Alicia

Choose friends who will help you do what is right!—Stephanie

Go to the school a couple of days before school starts. Take a look around so that when the first day comes, you will have a basic idea of where to go. Some schools even have maps. Don't be afraid to ask an older classmate for directions. They remember what it was like on the first day of school and will be happy to help.—Kaitlyn

Quiz: Pants on Fire?

by Susan Palacio

Liar, liar, _____ ___ ____!

I bet you could finish that sentence! We've all been guilty of lying. Saying we haven't would be . . . well, a lie! Take this quiz to see how close you are to the fire, so to speak.

You and your little brother sometimes argue. In the middle of a shoving match, a lamp gets knocked over and breaks. Mom takes you off by yourself to find out what happened. You say . . .

A) "Sorry Mom, Davis and I were fighting, and we knocked over a lamp and it broke. It is both our faults."

B) "Mooooom, Davis pushed me into the lamp, and it broke!"

C) "Davis broke the lamp. It was all his fault!"

You're walking to the lunchroom when your BFF starts talking about the most amazing pair of expensive jeans she just bought. As she models them, she comments on your jeans and asks where you bought them. You bought them at Walmart. You . . .

A) smile and say, "Actually, Walmart! Aren't they cute?"

B) shrug and comment, "I don't really remember."

C) look away and quickly say, "Oh, some store in the mall."

It's Friday night and your friend Ally has asked you to spend the night. You know Ally has also invited some older girls who sometimes get into trouble. You know your parents wouldn't approve if they knew. You . . .

A) tell your mom about the older girls anyway, and hope she still lets you go.

B) tell your mom Ally has invited some other friends to come over, but you don't tell her who.

C) only tell your mom Ally has invited you to spend the night and nothing else.

A group of totally cool girls are talking about a movie that recently came out. Noticing you are sort of listening, they ask if you liked the new movie. You haven't seen it because your mom said it was a little too mature. You don't want to get teased about it, so you say . . .

A) "I actually haven't seen it. Did you guys like it?"

B) "I haven't seen it, but I'm planning to see it soon. Tell me all about it!"

C) "Yeah, it was awesome!"

Your mom drops you off for school in plenty of time to make it to first period before the bell. On your way to class, you stop in the bathroom with one of your friends, start talking, and lose track of time. The late bell rings. You rush to class and tell the teacher . . .

A) "Sorry I'm late. I lost track of time."

B) "I was using the bathroom."

C) "My mom was a little late dropping me off today."

Your first-period teacher told you to study the chapter 3 summary to prepare for the test. You forgot and ended up with a D. School policy states that any grade below a C requires a parent's signature on the test. You . . .

A) Ask your mom or dad to sign the test and admit you forgot to study the summary. And promise you will do better the next time.

B) Ask your mom or dad to sign the test, and tell them almost everyone in class failed, which isn't exactly true.

C) Sign the test yourself. Your parents just won't understand, and besides, you would be grounded for life if they knew you failed.

Over summer vacation, you went to camp for a week. The first night, the camp counselor asked all sorts of group questions for everyone to answer. She asked, "Have you ever met any celebrities?" Almost everyone who answered before you said they had met a celebrity. You say . . .

A) "No! But I have a friend who saw one at the grocery store!"

B) "Yeah, I sorta met one through a friend."

C) "Yeah, I've met one. She shops at my grocery store. I see her all the time. She's so cool."

On her way out the door for a meeting, your mom asks you to clean your room because company is coming over for dinner. The minute she leaves, you grab a snack, turn on your tablet, and play for an hour straight. When Mom gets back, you quickly shut off the game before she sees you. When she asks why you haven't cleaned your room, you say . . .

A) "Sorry, Mom. I got caught up playing on my tablet. I'll go do it right now."

B) "I was working on something. I was going to do it next, I promise!"

C) "I couldn't find any of the cleaning supplies."

How did you score?

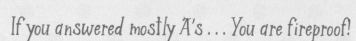

If you answered mostly A's . . . You are fireproof!

You know how to handle situations with grace and honesty. Instead of caring about what others think, you are more concerned about being truthful. Even though honesty is hard to practice, keep it up!

If you answered mostly B's . . . You are hot and cold!

Watch out! That fire alarm is about to go off. You have a hard time telling the *whole* truth. Sometimes being honest comes easily, but other times you slip up and lie. Watch out for situations where you know you are tempted to lie (exaggerating in a story, leaving out information you know you shouldn't, bending the truth, etc.). Telling half-truths is the same as telling a lie.

If you answered mostly C's . . . Stop, drop, and roll!

Your pants are on fire! You have some work to do on being honest. You tend to take the easy way out when difficult or tempting situations come around. Take some time and confess this to God. Then ask Him to help you tell the truth, even when it's not easy.

Would You Stand?
The Dilemma of Fitting In

by Vicki Courtney

When my youngest son was in high school, about three hundred students gathered together to vote on the theme for the homecoming dance. The homecoming dance is the most important dance *all* school year, so it gets a decorating theme. (Maybe your bedroom has a theme, like butterflies or peace signs.) At this meeting the students were given four choices for the theme (don't worry—butterflies was not one of them!). They were supposed to raise their hands when their favorite theme was called. I noticed a group of about ten girls whispering back and forth about which theme they would vote on. When it came time for the vote, and their choice was called, they all confidently raised their hands together. They were *convinced* this was the theme they wanted. As soon as their hands went in the air, they glanced around the room. Out of all those students, only a few other people liked that theme. Their choice was not

the popular one. A few of the girls became so uncomfortable that they lowered their hands before their vote was counted. They wanted to fit in so badly that they changed their vote just to go along with the crowd!

Almost every child, tween, teen, and even adult wants to fit in. Sooner or later, you will be faced with a moment when you will have to choose to fit in with the crowd or stand up for what you believe in. Standing up may be hard—and may even mean that you won't be popular. As a Christian, this can be a tough challenge if fitting in means going against your faith or belief in God. Believe it or not, the Bible contains a story about three teenagers who had to face that very challenge! And get this—standing up for what they believed almost cost them their lives.

Maybe you remember the story of Shadrach, Meshach, and Abednego. A foreign nation conquered their home, and they were taken away to a place called Babylon. This nation believed in different gods and didn't believe in the one true God. God told the boys not to worship any gods (or idols) except for Him.

King Nebuchadnezzar—the guy in charge of Babylon at the time—didn't believe in God. In fact, he made a gold statue that was ninety feet tall—that's about fifteen people your dad's height standing on each other's shoulders! The king told everyone to bow down to the idol whenever they heard the sound of the horn, flute, and harp, In other words, when the music started playing, hit the dirt! Then the king said that anyone who refused to fall down and worship the gold image would immediately be thrown into a blazing furnace. Imagine the heat from a fireplace or campfire. That furnace was like thousands and thousands of campfires put together. And believe me, the king wasn't planning to use the fire to roast marshmallows!

When the music began playing, everyone hit the dirt—except Shadrach, Meshach, and Abednego. They refused to bow down and worship the golden image. Someone told the king, and he asked to see the boys. (Don't you hate tattletales?) The king gave them one more chance to bow down and worship the golden image and reminded them that if they didn't, they would be tossed into the fiery furnace.

Now stop for a minute and think about their situation. It is normal to want to go along with what everyone else does. And it is even more normal to want to live! Yet these boys refused to follow the crowd and bow down to the image. Remember the girls voting on the homecoming theme? They caved into peer pressure with just three hundred other students. Picture a much, much larger group of people. And imagine these three boys standing while everyone else is bowing down. Would you have continued standing when the music played?

Fast-forward to when the king decides to give the guys one more chance to bow down and worship the idol. Now what would you do? Would you still be standing when the music began to play again? The Bible tells us what they said and did:

"Nebuchadnezzar, we don't need to give you an answer to this question. If the God we serve exists, then He can rescue us from the furnace of blazing fire, and He can rescue us from the power of you, the king. But even if He does not rescue us, we want you as king to know that we will not serve your gods or worship the gold statue you set up" (Daniel 3:16–18).

Wow! Forget the music, and send the orchestra home. These boys had made up their minds. They knew their God *could* rescue them, but they did not know whether He actually *would*. They were willing to stand up for God, even if it meant they might die. Most of us would have probably bowed down the second time after one look at that fiery furnace.

So what do you think happened to the boys? The Bible tells us that the king was so angry that he had the furnace heated up seven times hotter than before! It was so hot that the flames killed the soldiers who stood close the furnace. But it gets even worse. True to his promise, the king had the boys thrown into the fiery furnace.

But that's not the end of the story. Read what happens for yourself:

"He [the king] said, 'Look! I see four men walking around in the fire, unbound and unharmed, and the fourth looks like a son of the gods.' Nebuchadnezzar then approached the opening of the blazing furnace and shouted, 'Shadrach, Meshach and Abednego, servants of the Most High God, come out! Come here!'" (Daniel 3:25–26 NIV).

And the boys walked out of the fire. This is the stuff of headlines and social media. When the boys came out of the fiery furnace, they weren't harmed at all. In fact, not a hair on their heads was singed; their robes hadn't burned up, and the guys didn't even smell like a campfire. And that's not all. When the boys came out of the fire, the king knew that only the one true God could have saved them. Nebuchadnezzar's heart changed. He made a new law that anyone who said anything bad about the boys' God would be cut into pieces! Ewww!

I don't imagine you will be asked to bow down to a ninety-foot golden statue, but you will face plenty of other temptations on a daily basis. You'll be faced with standing up for what is right—or going along with what others do. What about gossip, lying, or disobeying your parents? What about wearing clothes that aren't modest? What about letting a friend cheat off your homework? What about saying bad words? Or even watching things on TV that you know your parents don't approve of?

When it comes to the temptation to "fit in," remember Shadrach, Meshach, and Abednego. They chose to stand up for God, and God blessed them. I can't promise that people won't make fun of you or that you'll become Miss Popular. I can promise that you will feel a lot better about yourself if you stand up for what you believe. And that's something nobody can take away from you.

In what ways have you felt pressure to fit in with the crowd? If everyone else is doing things that aren't pleasing to God, how do you handle that?

Scan for Video Answers!

You will feel a lot better about yourself if you stand up for what you believe.

Last Word on the World Around Me

"You are the salt of the earth. But if the salt should lose its taste, how can it be made salty? It's no longer good for anything but to be thrown out and trampled on by men. You are the light of the world. A city situated on a hill cannot be hidden. No one lights a lamp and puts it under a basket, but rather on a lampstand, and it gives light for all who are in the house. In the same way, let your light shine before men, so that they may see your good works and give glory to your Father in heaven."
—Matthew 5:13–16

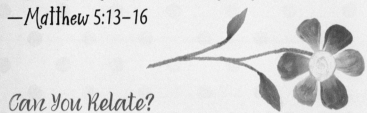

Can You Relate?

1. Do you think technology makes it hard to have real relationships with people? Why or why not? What can you do to make sure God remains your number-one priority?

2. Proverbs 18:21 says, "Life and death are in the power of the tongue, and those who love it will eat its fruit." What do you think that verse means? How can this verse influence the way you speak to others?

3. Proverbs 13:13 says, "The one who has contempt for instruction will pay the penalty, but the one who respects a command will be rewarded." Describe a time when it paid off to listen to good advice.

4. Do you have a Me-Monster? When does it come out? Read Matthew 22:37–39. How can that verse keep your Me-Monster away?

5. Philippians 2:5 says, "Make your own attitude that of Christ Jesus." How can you make your attitude more like Jesus?

6. Ephesians 4:26 (NIV) says, "Do not let the sun go down while you are still angry." How can that help you when it comes to arguments you may have with family and friends?

7. Matthew 5:44 says, "But I tell you, Love your enemies and pray for those who persecute you." Think of someone who has not been kind to you. Write out a prayer for this person.

8. Can you think of a time when you stood up for what you believed in (like Shadrach, Meshach, and Abednego) even though it wasn't the most popular decision? Describe what happened.

Jesus:
Why Should You Believe in Him?

Pretend your school is getting a new principal next week, and you and your friends decide to guess what the principal will be like to see who's the best guesser. You each make a list, and yours says,

- The principal is a woman named Elisa.
- She has red hair.
- She is from Omaha, Nebraska.
- She collects concert T-shirts.
- She owns a pet bulldog named Percy.
- She took a trip to Alaska last summer.

On the day the new principal arrives at school, you all meet after school to compare notes. After a few minutes, everybody turns to look at you. How is this possible? Every single one of your guesses is right. Your friends say you must've cheated. Maybe the principal is really your mom's old friend, or you read an article somewhere about her. But just then the principal stops by to introduce herself to your group, and she explains that there's no way for you to know all those facts about her.

Crazy story, huh? It could never happen because nobody could be *that* good at guessing. Unless you were omniscient (all knowing) like God—and you aren't!

Prophecies About Jesus

Predictive prophecies are facts about something that's going to happen in the future, and the Bible has a lot of them. Many of them are about Jesus and tell specific things about Him hundreds of years before He ever lived on the earth—long before anyone could cheat and make the right guesses. Way back in the days of the Old Testament, God told the people all about Jesus so they would recognize Him when He came to Earth.

The Bible's prophecies about Jesus include:

- He'd be born from a virgin.
- He'd be a descendant of Abraham and David.
- He would be born in Bethlehem but grow up in Nazareth.
- He would ride a donkey into Jerusalem.
- A friend would betray Him for thirty pieces of silver.
- He would be crucified.
- No bones would be broken at His death.

That's just eight of the fulfilled prophecies.

Think back to our story about the new principal. If there was no way you could ever guess about Elisa the principal and her bulldog Percy, then you can imagine there is no way a person living in the Old Testament could just randomly guess all those details about Jesus' life hundreds of years later. But God had a message He wanted to get out, and He is so much bigger and more amazing than we can imagine!

What the Prophecies Tell Us

Why did God give so many prophecies about His Son that all came true? Because this overwhelming evidence gives us confidence to believe that Jesus is who He said He is—the Son of God. And those fulfilled predictions give us confidence that Jesus did what He said He would do—save anyone who would believe in Him.

With all those predictions coming true, even the most doubtful person would have to admit that Jesus was more than just a good man.

He is your Savior.

Prophecies That Jesus Fulfilled

by Pam Gibbs

The Bible contains dozens of prophesies (predictions) about Jesus that He fulfilled while He lived. Here are just a few of them:

The Prophecy	Predicted in:	Fulfilled in:
He would be born in Bethlehem.	Micah 5:2	Luke 2:4–6
He would be a descendant of Isaac.	Genesis 17:19	Luke 3:34
He would be called Immanuel.	Isaiah 7:14	Matthew 1:23
He would live in Egypt a while.	Hosea 11:1	Matthew 2:13–15
He would speak in parables.	Psalm 78:2-4	Matthew 13:10–15
He would be declared the Son of God.	Psalm 2:7	Matthew 3:16–17
He would heal the brokenhearted.	Isaiah 61:1-2	Luke 4:18–19
He would be called King.	Zechariah 9:9	Mark 11:7–11

The Prophecy	Predicted in:	Fulfilled in:
He would be praised by children.	Psalm 8:2	Matthew 21:16
He would be betrayed.	Psalm 41:9	Luke 22:47–48
He would be silent when accused.	Isaiah 53:7	Mark 15:4–5
Soldiers would spit on Him and hit Him.	Isaiah 50:6	Matthew 26:67
He would be hated for no reason.	Psalm 35:19	John 15:18–25
He would be crucified with criminals.	Isaiah 53:12	Matthew 27:38
His hands and feet would be pierced.	Psalm 22:16	John 20:25–27
He would rise from the dead.	Psalm 49:15	Matthew 28:1–7

ABCs for Tween Girls

by Susie Davis

Before you ever learned to read, you learned the ABCs. As a tween, knowing some Bible ABCs is a must! Here you will find some verses that are important for every girl to know. Read through them. Then pick out your favorites and memorize them!

A good person produces good things from the treasury of a good heart, and an evil person produces evil things from the treasury of an evil heart.—Matthew 12:35 (NLT)

Be still, and know that I am God! I will be honored by every nation. I will be honored throughout the world!—Psalm 46:10

"Come to me, all of you who are weary and carry heavy burdens, and I will give you rest."—Matthew 11:28

Don't retaliate with insults when people insult you. Instead, pay them back with a blessing. That is what God has called you to do, and he will grant you his blessing.—1 Peter 3:9 (NLT)

Every word of God proves true.—Proverbs 30:5

Follow God's example, therefore, as dearly loved children.
—Ephesians 5:1 (NIV)

God is not a man, so he does not lie. He is not human, so he does not change his mind. Has he ever spoken and failed to act? Has he ever promised and not carried it through?
—Numbers 23:19 (NLT)

Happy is a man who finds wisdom and who acquires understanding, for she is more profitable than silver, and her revenue is better than gold. She is more precious than jewels; nothing you desire compares with her.
—Proverbs 3:13–15

If you believe, you will receive whatever you ask in prayer. —Matthew 21:22 (NIV)

Jesus told him, "I am the way, the truth, and the life. No one comes to the Father except through Me." —John 14:6

Keep your servant from deliberate sins! Don't let them control me. Then I will be free of guilt and innocent of great sin.
—Psalm 19:13 (NLT)

Lord, you alone are my inheritance, my cup of blessing; you guard all that is mine. —Psalm 16:5

My health may fail, and my spirit may grow weak, but God remains the strength of my heart; he is mine forever.
—Psalm 73:26

No one can serve two masters. For you will hate one and love the other; you will be devoted to one and despise the other. You cannot serve both God and money. —Matthew 6:24

O Lord, do not stay far away! You are my strength; come quickly to my aid! —Psalm 22:19

Please, LORD, rescue me! Come quickly, LORD, and help me. —Psalm 40:13

Better to hear the Quiet words of a wise person than the shouts of a foolish king. —Ecclesiastes 9:17

Rejoice with those who rejoice; weep with those who weep. —Romans 12:15

Seek the Kingdom of God above all else, and live righteously, and he will give you everything you need. —Matthew 6:33

The one thing I ask of the Lord, the thing I seek most, is to live in the house of the Lord all the days of my life delighting in the Lord's perfections. —Psalm 27:4

Under his wings you will find refuge; his faithfulness will be your shield and rampart. —Psalm 91:4

Victory comes from you, O Lord; may you bless your people. —Psalm 3:8 (NLT)

We know that everyone who has been born of God does not sin, but the One who is born of God keeps him, and the evil one does not touch him. —1 John 5:18

EXamine yourselves to see if your faith is genuine. Test yourselves. Surely you know that Jesus Christ is among you; if not, you have failed the test of genuine faith. —2 Corinthians 13:5 (NLT)

Yet you made them only a little lower than God and crowned them with glory and honor. —Psalm 8:5

Zeal is not good without knowledge, and the one who acts hastily sins. —Proverbs 19:2

Quiz: Who's in Charge of Your Life?

by Vicki Courtney

1. You are good at both dance and volleyball, but your parents won't let you do both because it will take up too much of your time. They tell you to choose one sport, but you don't want to make a decision you will regret. You . . .

A) make a list of the pros and cons of volleyball and dance. Dance wins. If you stick with it, you can be on the drill team, and that's what the popular girls do, right?

B) ask your three closest friends what you should pick and go with the majority. Besides, you don't want to pick one sport and then find out they chose the other one!

C) ask God to help you decide. God reminds you that some of the dance moves the older girls do in their performances are not appropriate. If you stick it out in dance, you might be faced with some tough decisions down the road.

2. A new girl at your church will be in your same grade at school. Your mom encourages you to invite her over to meet some of your friends. You . . .

A) grumble and complain because it will be so awkward. What will you talk about? What will your friends think?

B) tell your mom okay but call your friends and warn them in advance that it wasn't your idea. If they don't like the new girl, you won't either.

C) tell your mom it's a great idea. You can't imagine how it would feel to be in a new town and starting a new school and not know anyone.

3. Some of your friends are allowed on a social media site and want you to join too. You . . .

A) set up the account without telling your parents.

B) let your friends set up the account for you. That way, if mom and dad find out, you can blame your friends.

C) tell your friends you'll have to talk to your parents first and get their approval. Even if they say no, asking them is the right thing to do.

4. One of your friends asks if you are going to an upcoming party at another friend's house. At least you thought she was your friend—you weren't invited! You . . .

A) cry yourself to sleep that night. This girl has been tacky to you before, but there has to be a way to get invited to that party.

B) ask your mom to call the girl's mom and find out why you weren't invited. Who knows, maybe she can work her magic and get you an invitation to the party!

C) shed a few tears when you go to bed that night. You talk to God about how sad you are feeling and ask Him to help you deal with the disappointment. Who knows, maybe He's trying to protect you from something!

5. You try out for the lead in the upcoming school play, and everyone thinks you'll get the part. Small problem: the drama teacher's daughter is also trying out for the part. Sure enough, she gets it, even though she bombed her audition. You . . .

A) approach your drama teacher and tell her it's not fair. You are so much better than her daughter, and everyone else knows it.

B) call good ol' Mom. She can fix the problem!

C) pray about it and decide to trust God even when things aren't always fair. You ask Him to help you have a good attitude about the part you have been given and give it your best.

Total up your answers.
How many A's, B's, and C's did you have?

Self-paced program (Mostly A): You are in charge of your destiny. Doing what you want is more important than doing what God wants. However, when you take God out of the picture and run the show, you miss out on God's best. You need to do a serious heart check and start leaning on God more when making choices in life.

Friends and family plan (Mostly B): You rely on other people when making choices in life. Whether you're giving into peer pressure or counting on Mom to solve your problems, you've still taken the matter out of God's hands. Your friends and family can't possibly know you or the situation like God does. Sometimes God doesn't give us the answer we want to hear, but in the end God wants us to trust Him with the details.

Father knows best (Mostly C): When it comes to making choices, it looks like you are in the habit of letting God run the show. Good for you! When you are older and making important decisions—like your career and who you will marry—you will be more likely to rely on Him for wisdom. And you'll reap the benefits!

Trust in the Lord with all your heart, and do not rely on your own understanding; think about Him in all your ways, and He will guide you on the right paths.—Proverbs 3:5–6

Discovering What God Is Like

by Susan Palacio

Unscramble the words on the left to learn about the unique personality of God! Then match up the words with their definitions on the right. If you need help, turn to the Scripture reference in your Bible.

God is . . .

1. DINK _____ (Titus 3:4)

2. NGLOIV _____
   (1 John 4:7–8; Psalm 25:10)

3. HAFILUTF _____
   (Psalm 33:4; Psalm 36:5)

4. WFEPROLU _____
   (Psalm 77:13–14; Psalm 89:13;
   Psalm 145:6)

5. HWEEVRYEER _____
   (Psalm 139:7–12)

6. SIEW _____ (Romans 16:27)

7. YLHO _____ (Psalm 99:3–5)

8. AUCHNGGINN _____
   (Malachi 3:6)

9. UTTRH _____ (John 14:6)

10. ULMICERF _____
    (Ephesians 2:4)

a. not changing or capable of change; constant

b. showing gentle treatment of someone even if she doesn't deserve it; having compassion

c. wanting and liking to do good and to bring happiness to others; showing or growing out of gentleness or goodness of heart

d. full of influence; strong

e. being true or real

f. worthy of complete devotion and trust; set apart to the service of God

g. feeling or showing love; affectionate

h. good sense, or good judgment, sensible

i. in every place

j. loyal; firm in keeping promises; true to the facts

When You're Tempted by Your Friends

by Vicki Courtney

When I was in the fifth grade, a friend named Christy invited me to spend the night at her house. I had never been to her house before, so needless to say, I was pretty excited about the invitation. She also invited a girl named Julie, who was in our class. Our friendship had begun one afternoon when our teacher awarded us some free time at the end of the day. She handed out Tootsie Roll Pops to the entire class after we made all A's on a spelling test.

We were friends for a couple of months when I got the invitation to spend the night at Christy's house. My mom dropped me off on that Friday night after meeting Christy's mom. But there was a problem. Shortly after my mom left, Christy's mom also left and said she probably wouldn't be back until the next morning. I had never stayed in my own house alone at night, much less someone else's

house. When I asked Christy where her mom was going, she said her mom was going to her boyfriend's house to spend the night and shrugged it off like her departure was no big deal. Clearly, Christy had spent the night alone before now.

Julie showed up after Christy's mom left, and her mom didn't even come to the door, so she didn't know we were going to be alone. I remember thinking I should call my mom to come get me, but I didn't want the girls to think I was a scaredy-cat or a baby. They both seemed really comfortable staying there alone. I realized that Christy and Julie had a totally different home life than I did. Both of them lived with just their moms and had very little supervision. They could do just about anything they wanted, and they were accustomed to staying home alone, sometimes overnight.

A few hours after I got there, I experienced a Proverbs 1:10 moment, a situation in which I was "enticed by sin." Christy got a lighter and suggested that we light the cigarette butts her mom had left in an ashtray to see what smoking was like.

I am embarrassed to admit I gave into peer pressure that night, and I gave smoking a try. After choking and coughing so much I thought I'd die, I came to my senses and called my mom and asked her to come get me. I knew I was in over my head. I told the girls I didn't feel good, which was partially true after trying cigarettes.

After that night, my friendships with Christy and Julie became more distant. They were headed down a path I didn't want to go on, and I needed to find a new group of friends. Sadly, years later, they both struggled with drugs, and I was grateful for choosing a different path than theirs.

Can you think of a time when you have been tempted by sin? When someone encouraged you to do something wrong? Take a minute to talk with God and ask Him to give you the courage and strength to turn your back when others tempt you to sin. Ask Him to forgive you for times when you were the one who tempted others to sin.

Ask God to give you the courage and strength to turn your back when others tempt you to sin.

What God Wants to Tell You

I delight in you. (see Psalm 16:3)

Even if your father and mother abandon you,
I'll always love and keep you. (see Psalm 27:10)

I will counsel you and watch over you. (see Psalm 32:8)

I'll deliver you from all your fears. (see Psalm 34:4)

I'm close to you when you're brokenhearted. (see Psalm 34:18)

Delight yourself in me, and I will give you your heart's desires. (see Psalm 37:4)

I'm captivated by your beauty. (see Psalm 45:11)

I'll be your guide to the very end. (see Psalm 48:14)

I give you only good things. (see Psalm 84:11)

My love for you is higher than the heavens; My faithfulness reaches to the skies. (see Psalm 108:4)

My word helps you find your way, like a bright light on a dark path. (see Psalm 119:105)

I discipline you because I love you. (see Proverbs 3:12)

My name is a strong tower. Call to Me always and be safe. (see Proverbs 18:10)

Though your sins are red as scarlet, I will make them white as snow. (see Isaiah 1:18)

If you trust in Me, I will give you perfect peace. (see Isaiah 26:3)

I long to be gracious to you; I rise up to show you compassion. (see Isaiah 30:18)

I gather you in my arms and carry you close to My heart. (see Isaiah 40:11)

When you hope in Me, I will renew your strength. (see Isaiah 40:31)

Prayer Pop Quiz

by Vicki Courtney

1. *True or False:* God won't hear your prayers unless you are in church and you fold your hands and close your eyes.

2. *True or False:* The main reason we pray is to ask God for stuff.

3. *True or False:* The Lord's Prayer is a prayer Jesus taught His disciples to pray.

4. *True or False:* The Bible tells us that it's good to be show-offs when we pray and gather a big crowd around us and pray loudly.

5. *True or False:* The Bible says to pray for people who are mean to us or make fun of us.

6. *True or False:* Sometimes God is too busy to hear our prayers.

7. *True or False:* The Bible tells us that if we are suffering (struggling, hurting, etc.), we should pray.

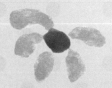

ANSWERS:

1. **False**. You can pray anytime and anywhere. Jeremiah 29:12 says, "You will call to Me and come and pray to Me, and I will listen to you." God tells us to call to Him through prayer whenever we need Him, and He will listen.

2. **False**. Prayer is about communicating with God and growing closer to Him. We should always pray with an attitude that says, "Your kingdom come, Your will be done on earth as it is in heaven."

3. **True**. Matthew 6:9–13 says, "Therefore, you should pray like this: Our Father in heaven, your name be honored as holy. Your kingdom come. Your will be done on earth as it is in heaven. Give us today our daily bread. And forgive us our debts, as we also have forgiven our debtors. And do not bring us into temptation, but deliver us from the evil one. For Yours is the kingdom and the power and the glory forever. Amen."

4. **False**. Matthew 6:5–6 says, "Whenever you pray, you must not be like the hypocrites, because they love to pray standing in the synagogues and on the street corners to be seen by people. I assure you: They've got their reward! But when you pray, go into your private room, shut your door, and pray to your Father who is in secret. And your Father who sees in secret will reward you."

5. **True**. Matthew 5:44–45 says, "But I tell you, love your enemies and pray for those who persecute you, so that you may be sons of your Father in heaven."

6. **False**. First John 5:14 says, "Now this is the confidence we have before Him: whenever we ask anything according to His will, He hears us."

7. **True**. James 5:13 says, "Is anyone among you suffering? He should pray. Is anyone cheerful? He should sing praises."

Creative Ways to Connect with God

by Susan Palacio

When I was growing up, communicating with others was limited to face-to-face conversations, letters in the mail, or phone calls on a home telephone that was attached by a cord running into the wall!

Today there are a gazillion other ways to communicate with people instantly through texts, social media, and apps on your phone or tablet. Just as you have lots of options for talking with your friends, the same is true of God. Prayer is one way to talk to God, but there are also lots of other ways to grow and show your faith in Him, none of which involve a digital device!

Start by picking an activity you naturally like to do, like singing or painting. Then think of a way you can talk to God by doing that activity. For the artist, maybe it's painting things you see outside that remind you God is the ultimate Creator (skies, mountains, or flowers). As you paint, thank God for being a creative God. For the singer, maybe you could make up praise songs when you're in the shower.

> Let them praise
> His name with dancing
> and make music to Him
> with tambourine and lyre.
> —Psalm 149:3

Here are some other creative ways to connect with God:

If drawing's your thing:

- Make a "thank You" card to God and draw the things that you are grateful for in your life.
- Create a poster/sign and write this sentence at the top: "I am happy that God made me the way I am" or "I am fearfully and wonderfully made." Then draw unique character traits God has given you (your talents, your physical features, and personality traits)

If writing's your thing:

- Write in a journal a top ten list of reasons you love God.
- List words describing God starting with each letter of the alphabet.
- Write about a Bible story as if you were one of the characters (what you may have felt, heard, or seen). For example, you could write from Jonah's perspective when he was in the belly of the whale.

If collages are your thing:

- Cut out magazine words that describe how you view God or feel about Him (Friend, Father, love, wonderful, etc.). Then create a poster with those words, and put a picture of you in the middle to show how God surrounds you in His love.
- Create a scrapbook page filled with pictures of friends or family who don't know Jesus yet. Then pray for them!
- Get a canvas and decorate it with your favorite Bible verses. (Verses work really well as borders too!)

If dancing's your thing:

- Make up a dance to your favorite praise song. Then dance for Him. (Don't worry, no one is watching.)
- Create a dance to represent the different days of creation.
- Create a ballet dance that shows how you can dance before God the King.

If crafts are your thing:

- Create a piece of art that reminds you of God. You could make a popsicle-stick cross or decorate a flowerpot that reminds you to keep growing in your faith (see Luke 2:52)!
- Make a bookmark with your favorite Bible verse on it.

- Decorate a box or other container and use it to collect your change to give to a local charity. Jesus tells us to take care of the poor!

If poetry's your thing:

- Write a poem that tells the story of your love for Him. (Rhyming is not required!)
- Write a poem describing what you hope heaven is like.

If singing's your thing:

- Make up a song to your favorite verse in the Bible. Try looking in Psalms for some lyrics.
- Choose a favorite church hymn and try singing the lyrics with a new, updated rhythm.

If beading's your thing:

- Make a bracelet with beads to represent the fruit of the Spirit (see Galatians 5:22–23). Every time you wear it, ask God to help you develop those traits in your life.
- Use letter beads that spell out some of the different names for Jesus, such as *Prince of Peace* or *Son of God*, and create a necklace that will be a great conversation starter for talking about Him.

Where to Go When . . .

You are discouraged. . . . Psalm 34

You feel sad. . . . John 14:1-4

God feels far away. . . . Psalm 139:1-12

You are sick. . . . Psalm 41

Others disappoint you. . . . Psalm 27

You have sinned. . . . Psalm 51

You need direction. . . . Proverbs 3:1-6

You are anxious. . . . Philippians 4:6-7

You need courage. . . . Joshua 1:1-9

You need comfort. . . . 2 Corinthians 1:3-4

You need hope. . . . Psalm 34:18

A friend has betrayed you. . . . Psalm 55

You are traveling. . . . Psalm 121

You are tired. . . . Psalm 127:1-2

You are waiting on God. . . . Psalm 130:5

You are prideful. . . . Proverbs 11:2

You don't know what to pray. . . . Matthew 6:5-15

You look down on others. . . . Matthew 7:1-5

You have turned away from God. . . . Luke 15:11-32

You want to get revenge. . . . Romans 12:19

You are afraid of death. . . . 1 Corinthians 15:54-57

You feel like you don't make a difference. . . . Galatians 6:9

You are in a spiritual battle. . . . Ephesians 6:10-18

You have lost a loved one. . . . 1 Thessalonians 4:13-18

You are facing temptation. . . . 1 Corinthians 10:13

You doubt God's love for you. . . . John 3:16

You feel weary. . . . Matthew 11:28-30

You are selfish. . . . 2 Corinthians 9:7

You want to stay on the right path. . . . Psalm 119:9-11

You are worried about finances. . . . Matthew 6:25-34

You are carrying a grudge. . . . Ephesians 4:25-32

You are worried about the future. . . . Jeremiah 29:11

You are tempted to act like the world. . . . Romans 12:2

Giving God the Respect He Deserves

by Vicki Courtney

When my daughter was in second grade, she was chosen to perform on a competitive cheer squad for a spring show at a local high school. She was the youngest member of the group. One afternoon when I picked her up from practice, she was especially quiet on the way home. Sensing something was not quite right, I asked her if anything happened during practice. She burst into tears and said the song they were using in the performance said "something very, very bad," and she was afraid if she told me, I would not let her be in the performance.

This was just days before the performance, and since my daughter was a flier (the one who gets tossed into the air), I couldn't really take her off the team. I assured her she could still perform. She went on to tell me some of the words in the song were "sooooooo bad" and she didn't want to say them out loud. Finally I convinced her that it was okay to tell me the words. Hesitantly, she leaned over and very quietly whispered the bad words she had heard in the song: "Oh my God." The song used that phrase in a sarcastic tone, and my daughter knew it was wrong to use God's name in that manner.

I was proud of my daughter for responding to the lyrics with a tender respect for God at such a young age. She was demonstrating the "fear of the LORD" described in Proverbs 9:10. To fear the Lord means having a deep respect and reverence for God. If you look up *reverence* in the dictionary, you will find this: "A feeling of profound awe and respect and often love; showing respect, especially a bow or curtsy."* I love that last definition: "a bow or curtsy."

That last part reminds me of seeing people bow or curtsy in the presence of nobility (a king or queen) as a sign of respect. How much more does the God of the universe deserve our respect? While we don't usually bow or curtsy in the Lord's presence, we can learn to bow our hearts and our actions in honor of our Creator.

---

* The American Heritage® Dictionary of the English Language, Fourth Edition Copyright © 2006 by Houghton Mifflin Company. Published by Houghton Mifflin Company. All rights reserved.

Here are some ways we can bow our hearts and show a proper fear of the Lord:

- Never use the Lord's name in vain. This includes phrases like: "Oh my God!" and "Jesus Christ!" that are often spoken in a disrespectful manner.

- Never joke around during prayer time. Focus your attention on the words being spoken.

- Participate in singing when worshipping in church rather than merely moving your lips.

- Don't talk or fidget during the church service. This also includes writing notes to friends, checking your cell phone for messages, texting, and other distractions.

How are you doing when it comes to giving God the honor and respect He deserves?

Chances are, we all have room for improvement.

The fear of the Lord is the beginning of wisdom, and the knowledge of the Holy One is understanding.
—Proverbs 9:10

Quiz: My Way vs. the High Way

by Susan Palacio

Have you ever seen a boxing match? Okay, well maybe not a whole match, but you've probably at least caught a glimpse of the boxing ring with two boxers, each in opposite corners. These two will fight to determine who is the biggest, strongest, best. In the same way, you have a boxing match going on in your life. It's between the "high way" and "my way."

The "high way" is listening to God, the Bible, and godly people to help you make decisions. God has placed people in our lives to help instruct us how to live. Those people of authority or power (like your parents, pastor, and teachers) in your life usually know what they are talking about, and it's important to listen to them. The "my way" is just that—you want to do things *your way*. You don't want to listen to God or anyone else when it comes to making decisions. You want to make your own choices without anybody giving you advice.

Let's see whether the "high way" or "my way" is in control of your life. For each of the statements below, rate yourself by selecting a number that best describes how you typically behave. The closer you circle a number to the left (or toward the 1) means that sentence does not describe you at all. The further you are to the right (or toward 10), the more the sentence describes you. A score of 5 or 6 would mean you fall somewhere in the middle.

I always read the directions on tests or homework assignments.

1   2   3   4   5   6   7   8   9   10

When Mom offers help on a project I'm working on, I listen to her suggestions.

1   2   3   4   5   6   7   8   9   10

When a family member warns me about something (like a boy or a movie), I listen.

1   2   3   4   5   6   7   8   9   10

I pay attention to teachers when they tell me things I need to work on.

1   2   3   4   5   6   7   8   9   10

If my parents tell me to put on a jacket because it's cold, I go grab one.

1   2   3   4   5   6   7   8   9   10

When I'm frustrated because I can't do something well, I find somebody who can coach me on doing it right and correcting my mistakes.

1   2   3   4   5   6   7   8   9   10

I make an effort to learn the Bible, God's ultimate instruction manual.

1   2   3   4   5   6   7   8   9   10

If Mom tells me it's not smart to purchase something, I don't spend my money on it.

1   2   3   4   5   6   7   8   9   10

While playing sports, if my coach gives me direction, I listen and change how I'm playing.

1   2   3   4   5   6   7   8   9   10

In church, I pay attention to lessons and try to learn how to live a godly life.

1   2   3   4   5   6   7   8   9   10

Now add up all your circled numbers, and see how you scored.

If you scored between 10 and 39,

you're following the High Way! When it comes to listening to advice of those in authority, you allow them to walk on the road with you. You understand the wisdom of listening to those who have been there, done that. Instead of letting your own plans and desires win out, you make wise choices and usually benefit from them.

If you scored between 40 and 70,

you're in the middle of the road. Even though you sometimes take the good advice of others, you still have a stubborn streak that causes you to choose your own way. Next time someone in authority (like a parent or teacher) gives you instruction, try listening to that advice and giving it a try. Even though someone's advice may not always work out, be open to it.

If you scored between 71 and 100,

then you're screaming "my way!" When you hear advice, you tend to quickly do the opposite. Instead of caring about what might be wise, you prefer to blaze your own trail, which often leads to heartache. God has placed authority figures in your life for a reason, so start opening your ears and your heart!

Just Ask!
Your Questions Answered

by Vicki Courtney

Q. *How many people can fit into heaven?*
(Catherine, age 8)

A. Since God created heaven, it will be plenty big enough to hold all those who believe in His Son, Jesus! In fact, the Bible tells us there are many mansions, and God prepares a place for each of us.

Q. *Why doesn't God answer some prayers?* (Megan, age 9)

A. God always answers prayer. He just doesn't always answer in the way we want.
When we pray, God says "yes," "no," or "wait." We might not agree with the way He answers, but we can trust that He is doing what is best for us.

Q. *Why does God like some people more than other people?* (Mikayla, age 10)

A. God loves us all just the same. I know it's hard to believe since people usually have favorites. You know how some teachers seem to like the smart kids in the class better? God is not like that. He doesn't even like the ones who are serving Him better than the ones who are not. God created each and every one of us, and even though we sometimes disappoint Him, He never stops loving us. He loves you just as much as He loves your pastor. Pretty amazing, huh?

Q. When is the rapture coming?
(Alexandra, age 10)

A. When Jesus lived on the earth (as a man), He told His disciples that He would someday return again and that His return would signal the end of the world. The word we use for the return of Jesus is rapture. This is how the Bible describes the rapture in Matthew 24:30–31:

"Then the sign of the Son of Man will appear in the sky, and then all the peoples of the earth will mourn; and they will see the Son of Man coming on the clouds of heaven with power and great glory. He will send out His angels with a loud trumpet, and they will gather His elect from the four winds, from one end of the sky to the other."

One day the disciples asked Jesus if there would be some kind of sign to when the end of the world would take place. In Matthew 24, Jesus told them that there would be signs like famines (starvation), earthquakes, and wars around the world. He also said that sin would be everywhere. False prophets (people who claim to know God's truth but are fakes) would be everywhere. Finally, He said that the gospel (the message that Jesus died on the cross for our sins) would be preached everywhere before the end of the world. He reminded the disciples that even when all those signs occurred, He might not return right away.

The end of the world may or may not happen in your lifetime. It may be hundreds or even thousands of years away. The most important thing Jesus tells us about His return is to be ready. If you are a Christian, you are prepared. His future return should inspire us to tell other people about Him so they can go to heaven too.

Q. How did the people who wrote the Bible know what to write? (Anna, age 11)

A. That's a great question! The Bible has many writers, but God is the one who gave them the message they wrote down, and He protected the message from error. Second Timothy 3:16 says,

"All Scripture is inspired by God and is profitable for teaching, for rebuking, for correcting, for training in righteousness." In order for the Bible to be true, it had to come from God!

There are two different ways God inspired the writers. First, He spoke to them directly. In the Old Testament, or first part of your Bible, God often spoke out loud to certain people, like Moses or the prophets, and those people wrote down what He said. In the first four books of the New Testament (the Gospels), people recorded Jesus' actual words. Those are examples of God directly speaking to people. Second, God inspired people indirectly by putting thoughts in their minds. Have you ever had a great idea pop into your mind out of nowhere? That's sort of how God worked with other writers in the Bible. He gave them the message in their minds, and they wrote them down. The cool thing is this: Even though forty different people wrote the Bible over fifteen hundred years, the theme is the same throughout the whole book: God loves you and sent His Son to save you.

Q. *How can God be everywhere at one time?* (Tiffany, age 11)

A. That is another one of the mysteries of God. No matter how hard we try to understand it, we can't. Our brains just can't figure it out. However, nothing is impossible with God. That's what makes Him God! He is omniscient (all-knowing) and omnipresent (everywhere at once) and omnipotent (all-powerful). This can give us great comfort. Whenever and wherever we need Him, He is there. And nothing is too big for Him to handle.

Q. *Did God make dinosaurs, and why are they not in the Bible?* (Bridgette, age 11)

A. Yes! Genesis tells us that on day six, God created all land animals, and that includes dinosaurs. Some people think that dinosaurs are mentioned in the Bible. For instance, some Hebrew words like Tanniyn, Behemoth, and Leviathan found in the Old Testament may refer to dinosaurs (Job 40:15–24; Job 41; Psalm 104:25–26; Isaiah 27:1).

Q. Will God heal my arthritis? I have faith in God. (Kaylee, age 10)

A. Kaylee, one of the girls in my office has arthritis, so I asked her to answer your question. Here is what she had to say:

You know what, Kaylee? I want to know that very thing myself! When I was just a little older than you, my doctor told me that I had arthritis too. It hurt so bad, and I wanted the pain to go away. And I really wanted to know if I was going to have arthritis forever! My mom and I would pray for healing, but we also believed that God had a purpose for my arthritis. Over the years, God has not healed my body (yet), but He has given me so much more! I have learned how to stay strong through really tough times. In James 1:2–4, the Bible says, "Consider it a great joy, my brothers, whenever you experience various trials, knowing that the testing of your faith produces endurance. But endurance must do its complete work, so that you may be mature and complete, lacking nothing."

That verse means that by making it through rough times in life (like physical pain), God is making you more like Him. Your life can be an encouragement to others around you too. Keep the faith, Kaylee. Even if God does not heal your body (and I pray He will!), remember that He loves you no matter what. He is good.

Q. Do you eat in heaven? (Hannah, age 12)

A. In heaven we won't have bodies like we do now. The Bible talks about our bodies being like a "tent" (2 Corinthians 5:4). That verse also says we will get rid of our bodies when we die and exchange them for a new "heavenly body." I'm not sure what that really means, but I doubt we will need to eat! I know it's hard to imagine what heaven will be like since earth is all we know. Sometimes I joke about my "mansion" in heaven and that I hope I can have my very own Starbucks coffee shop in it! I love grande vanilla lattes, but truthfully, I won't need Starbucks to be happy when I'm in heaven. I will have Jesus, and that's all I need.

Quiz: What Does It Mean to Be a Christian?

by Susie Davis

Did you know there is a difference between *being* a Christian and *acting* like a Christian? A lot of people can *act* like Christians, but there's only one way to become a Christian. What is that one thing? Take this pop quiz to see if you know!

True or False . . .

True	False	1.	You are a Christian if you go to church.
True	False	2.	You are a Christian if you are really nice to other people.
True	False	3.	You are a Christian if you pray (even if it is just at mealtimes).
True	False	4.	You are a Christian if you obey your parents.
True	False	5.	You are a Christian if you read your Bible.
True	False	6.	You are a Christian if you do good things and are a good person.
True	False	7.	You are a Christian if you confess your sins to God.
True	False	8.	You are a Christian if you memorize Bible verses.
True	False	9.	You are a Christian if your parents are Christians.
True	False	10.	You are a Christian if you believe that Jesus died on the cross for your sins and trust in Him to be your Savior.

Answers:
1–9: False   10: True

If you answered true to any question 1–9, you are not alone. Most people believe that those are the things that make someone a Christian, but they don't. Being a Christian and acting like a Christian are important, but only one will give you eternal life in heaven. Let me explain.

Acting Like a Christian:

Most of the things listed in questions 1–9 are actions that Christians often show. However, lots of non-Christians do those things too. They may go to church on Sundays, pray at meals, and even read the Bible every now and then.

However, when you become a Christian, you will discover that the actions in questions 1–9 come out of your love for God and your appreciation for His gift of eternal life. In fact, the Bible says the only way we can truly love other people is because He loved us first!

Being a Christian:

When you make the decision to trust in Jesus to save you, what you are saying is this: "Jesus, I believe You died on the cross for my sins, and I know that if I turn from my sin and trust in You, I can have eternal life in heaven with You. Only You could save me from my sins. I believe there is nothing I can do on my own to earn the right to go to heaven. I want to serve You with my life."

The decision to become a Christian is a choice only you can make. Your parents can't make the choice for you. Your pastor can't decide for you. Neither can your Sunday school teacher or best friend.

It's your choice.

What will you decide?

Sharing Your Faith

Do you want to share your faith with a friend, but you're not sure how to get started?

Here are a few steps to steer you in the right direction.

1. Pray first. Ask for God's wisdom, strength, and courage to share about Jesus.

2. Watch for clues from your friend, such as if she asks where you go to church or how you manage to be nice to that one kid at school who drives everyone else crazy. If a friend doesn't seem interested in talking about religious stuff, don't force her. And don't take it personally—it's God's job to change hearts. Just keep praying for her and for other opportunities to talk about your faith.

3. Answer her questions about what makes you different, then ask her a question like one of the following:

Do you have any special beliefs about God or Jesus?

Do you believe in a heaven and a hell?

When you die, where do you think you'll go?

4. If your friend seems interested in continuing to talk, you can . . .
- explain how you came to believe in Jesus, how He has changed your life, and how He wants to change her life too.
- tell her about Jesus dying on the cross and how He wants to have a personal relationship with her.

- share some Bible verses with her that you wrote down beforehand. Some great verses you can choose from are Romans 6:23; John 14:6; Romans 10:9–10; 1 John 5:11–13; John 5:24; and Ephesians 2:8–9.

Emphasize that being a Christian is a lifetime relationship with Jesus, not just a casual momentary event. If she is still interested in talking more, move on to the next step.

If your friend answers yes to these questions, then lead her in a prayer to accept Christ.

If you start into any of these areas and get stumped by questions, tell your friend she can talk to someone you know (at home or church) for more help, then invite her to visit that person with you as soon as possible.

5. Ask some questions to find out if she is ready and wants to become a Christian.

Do you understand that sin separates us from God and that you are a sinner?

Do you believe that Jesus died on the cross for your sins and rose from the grave for you?

Do you want a friendship with Jesus?

Are you willing to make Jesus the Lord of your life?

Are you ready to invite Jesus into your life now?

God Is Not a Vending Machine

by Vicki Courtney

Have you ever stayed in a hotel? You know how they have soda machines and icemakers on almost every floor? Have you noticed the machines that have all the snacks? All you have to do is put in your money and make your selection. D–5. B-2. Then those peanut-butter crackers or M&Ms are all yours. It's that easy!

Sometimes we can treat praying kind of like a vending machine. We give God our prayers, and we expect Him to give us what we ask for. Only prayer doesn't really work that way. Let me tell you a little about how I learned about prayer.

When I was little, I used to pray "wish prayers" to God. They were kind of like quarters I would put in the vending machine, hoping I would get what I punched in. "God, I'll take an A on my test tomorrow." And each night I went over my list of wishes with God. It went something like this:

Dear God,
Please, please, please help me remember my spelling words even though I didn't really study. And please let Mark like me and not Missy. And please make my brother vanish into thin air. Amen.

As I went on to middle school, my prayers were still a lot about what I wanted: making the cheerleading squad, winning track meets, getting invited to the cool kids' houses, and praying my parents wouldn't find out I got in trouble for passing notes in class.

By high school it was clear that God didn't always answer my prayers the way I wanted. I pretty much decided that He either (a) must not be listening to me or (b) must not care. Either way, I didn't think that prayer worked, so my prayers basically stopped except for when I was in real big trouble. Then I might say a prayer to see if I got any results.

When I became a Christian in my college years, I figured out that I had a lot to learn about prayer. Someone taught me the ACTS model of prayer. ACTS stands for Adoration, Confession, Thanks, and Supplication. The first letter of each word spells out the word acts. People of any age can use this model. In fact, I still use this method today.

The ACTS Prayer Model:

ADORATION

The A of ACTS stands for *adoration*. Adoration simply means to brag on God. We should start prayer by praising God for how awesome He is. When you pray, start by remembering what you love about God, and adore Him for those things. Examples would be praising Him for His perfection, His enormous power, His ability to forgive us, His control of all the earth and the skies, His desire to love us completely, and His gift of Jesus. The list goes on and on! You can praise God for anything. Praising God helps us take the focus off ourselves and direct our attention to God.

CONFESSION

The C of ACTS stands for *confession*. Confession is basically telling God when we've done something wrong and feel sorry for it. When I get to the confession part of my prayer time, I try to think of specific ways I have been wrong rather than simply saying "Forgive me for my sins." An example would be: "Lord, I confess I was wrong when I had a bad attitude today when my mom asked me to unload the dishwasher."

If my confession involves a sin against another person, like my mom, God often uses my prayer time to direct me to talk to that person and ask for his or her forgiveness. As you confess your sins to God, remember that no sin is too big for Him to forgive. Our part is to admit our sin. His part is forgiveness (see 1 John 1:9).

THANKS

The T in ACTS stands for *thanksgiving*. I bet you can think of one holiday when it is easy to remember to thank God for His blessings. I love Thanksgiving not only because of the turkey and pumpkin pie feast, but also because, as a family, we offer thanks to God for what He has given us.

We also thank Him for the prayers He has answered (even if it wasn't the answer we wanted). Did you know that we are supposed to have Thanksgiving all year long? That's right! Every day should be Thanksgiving, with or without the turkey and dressing. It's easy to forget to thank God on a regular basis. One way to remember is to use a prayer journal. Start by taking a notebook, journal, or even a piece of paper and make a list of things you are thankful for, like your church, your friends, your parents, or your brothers or sisters (yes, even though they drive you crazy!). If you can't think of anything, you should always be thankful for God's Son, Jesus, who died on the cross for you. With all that we have been blessed with, we should have no problem thinking of things to thank God for.

In addition to thanking God for His blessings, we can also thank Him for answering our prayers. Begin by taking that same journal and dividing the pages into two columns. In one column, list your prayer requests. In the other column, list how or when God answered your prayer, even if the answer was no. The Bible tells us to thank God in all circumstances. Check out 1 Thessalonians 5:18.

SUPPLICATION

The S in ACTS stands for *supplication*. That means asking God for something for ourselves or for others. When you ask God for things, try to think of others first. Tell God about your own needs last. This is the part of the prayer when you talk to God about your grandmother who is sick, or your dad who needs a new job, or maybe your best friend whose parents are divorcing. After you pray for others, then pray about your own needs. Be honest with God. Are you sad? Tell Him. Are you scared? Tell Him. Talk to Him like you would talk to your very best friend. Remember that your prayers are heard. Sometimes God doesn't answer our prayers in the way we would like. Like the time I prayed and prayed to make the cheerleading squad in seventh grade, but I didn't. Now I understand that God's plans are better than my plans.

So, what about you? Do you treat God like a vending machine? If so, you are missing out on what prayer is all about. Put your change away and use the ACTS model to pray. Talk to God on a daily basis. You don't have to wait until bedtime to say your prayers. Get used to talking to Him throughout the day as things come up. He can't wait to talk to you.

Never Evers with God

Never Ever forget that God loves you.

Never Ever believe that God will stop loving you.

Never Ever forget that God happily forgives you when you ask.

Never Ever think you can make God forget about you.

Never Ever believe the lie that you have to be perfect for God to love you.

Never Ever feel like you have to ask God over and over to save you. Once is enough.

Never Ever believe that the devil is stronger than God.

Never Ever forget God has assigned angels to watch over you.

Never Ever forget the Bible will help you with your everyday problems.

The Character of God

The Bible highlights different aspects of God's personality. Match the Scripture in the left-hand column with the correct character of God listed in the right-hand column.

_____ 1. Genesis 1:1

_____ 2. Exodus 3:7–8

_____ 3. Deuteronomy 9:5

_____ 4. Psalm 23:4

_____ 5. Psalm 119:24

_____ 6. Proverbs 2:6

_____ 7. Jeremiah 18:6

_____ 8. Psalm 121:5

_____ 9. Matthew 1:23

_____ 10. Luke 15:2

_____ 11. John 8:12

_____ 12. Psalm 103:3

_____ 13. Psalm 37:26

_____ 14. Galatians 5:1

_____ 15. Luke 1:72

_____ 16. 2 Thessalonians 3:3

_____ 17. Hebrews 4:15

_____ 18. 1 John 4:8

_____ 19. 2 Samuel 22:33

a. Faithful

b. Sympathizer

c. With us

d. Generous

e. Wisdom

f. Freedom-giver

g. Rescuer

h. Counselor

i. Strong refuge

j. Merciful

k. Creator

l. Forgiver

m. Love

n. Comforter

o. Promise-keeper

p. Friend of sinners

q. Light of the world

r. Protector

s. Potter

Which of the above characteristics of God means something to you today? Why is that characteristic meaningful to you right now?

Sleep On It:
Good Advice for Making Decisions

by Vicki Courtney

Sometimes I put a Post-it note on my laptop that says, "Sleep on it." When I get stressful phone calls or e-mails and it would be easy to respond immediately without thinking through the consequences, the note reminds me to wait. I learned this little trick from my co-workers who started putting the Post-it notes on their monitors to remind them to think and pray for at least one night before making a big decision or responding to a difficult situation.

My Post-it note saved me once when I received a difficult call from a woman who wanted to come to one of my events. She left an angry voicemail message saying that when she went to register for the event online, she discovered it was already sold out. I was super mad when I heard her message because I couldn't understand why she was calling and blaming me for the fact that she

didn't register for the event in time. However, I practiced the Post-it note wisdom and decided to sleep on it before calling her back. The next day, she ended up leaving another message before I could call her back. This time she apologized for her attitude on the day before. Good thing I slept on it and didn't call her back in the midst of my anger.

Proverbs 14:15 says, "The inexperienced one believes anything, but the sensible one watches his steps." If you look the word *prudent* up in the dictionary, you might find something like: "wise, careful, using good judgment." God wants us to be careful when making decisions. When I was in fifth grade, a bunch of my friends were signing up to play soccer. I was into gymnastics, and I really enjoyed it. However, I wanted to do what my friends were doing, so I begged my mom to let me sign up for the soccer team.

She tried to talk me out of it since I was already in gymnastics, but I wouldn't listen. I signed up, bought the uniform and a brand new pair of cleats, and headed off to practice. After one practice I decided I absolutely *hated* playing soccer, but my mom made me keep my commitment. I got tired trying to play two sports and dreaded every soccer practice. I sat on the sidelines during most of the games anyway because I wasn't very good. If I had taken the time to "consider my steps" and think about the decision, I would have made a wiser choice.

As you get older, many of the decisions you will face will be more serious than whether or not to play on a soccer team. Maybe you'll say "yes" to dating too soon or cave into peer pressure to gossip about a girl. Maybe you'll react to a mean girl and lash out in anger. If you start following the proverb to "carefully consider your steps," chances are, you'll be more likely to make wiser choices when the big decisions come your way in the years to come.

Most importantly, when you wait before making a decision and sleep on it, you can talk to God about it and get His opinion. In the end, His wisdom is what really matters.

In the end, His wisdom is what really matters.

Gotta-Know Facts About the Bible

1. The Bible was written by at least forty different authors who were inspired by the Holy Spirit to write their stories.

2. The Bible is a collection of sixty-six books. There are thirty-nine Old Testament books and twenty-seven New Testament books.

3. The Bible tells one main story from Genesis to Revelation—God's rescue mission for sinners.

4. The Bible was the first-ever major printed and distributed book (around the year 1450).

5. The Bible is the all-time best-selling book in history.

6. The Bible has been translated into more than 1,200 languages—more than any other book ever written.

7. The Bible is unlike any other book because it is inerrant (without error), authoritative (over and above any other teaching), and sufficient (all that we need).

8. You can read the Bible out loud in about seventy hours.

9. The Bible contains about 775,000 words.

10. The longest name in the Bible is Mahershalalhashbaz (Isaiah 8:1). It has eighteen letters!

Ways to Pray

When you care about someone, you talk to that person. Think about how many times you talk to your closest friend each week. You most likely turn to that friend for advice, to vent, and to share exciting or awful news about your life. You also probably listen to that friend too, not only about her take on what you shared with her, but also about what is going on in her life. Relationships require two-way communication, and that communication is vital to having a healthy relationship.

Communicating with God is similar. He speaks, through His Word, and hopefully we listen. We speak to Him through prayer, and He definitely listens. Simply put, prayer is talking to God. He already knows our circumstances, thoughts, joys, frustrations, and concerns, but we talk to Him to hand over all that is going on in our lives and to praise Him for who He is. There are no special formulas or rules for how to talk to God, but here are some ideas for talking to the One who cares the most for you.

Creative Ways to Talk to God

- Make a list of some of the different names used for God in Scripture. Pick one and thank God for how He fulfills that name.

- Write a poem or a song praising God.

- Go outside during your favorite part of the day and thank God for His creation.

- Get a journal (or use your computer), and keep a written record of prayers. You'll be amazed at how God has worked in your life when you go back and read through those prayers.

- Write down the names of the people in your inner circle—close friends, family members, teammates—on index cards (one name per card), hole punch the index cards, and hook them on a ring. Pray for one person throughout the day. When you get through all the names, start all over again.

- Read a psalm a day, and let that prayer be your prayer throughout the day.

- Keep all the Christmas cards sent to your family each year, and pray for one family per day.

- At Thanksgiving, have everyone in your family list all that they were thankful for that particular year on little cut-out pieces of paper (one item per piece). Hole punch each piece, then run a ribbon through them and hang them on your Christmas tree.

- Have one person in your life you can pray with once a week, picking a day and time that works for you both. Your prayer time can be in person or over the phone (voice-to-voice, not through texts).

Survey: What Would You Ask God?

We asked girls your age this question: If you could ask God one question and get an answer right away, what would it be?

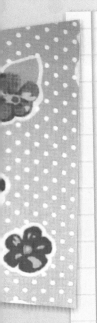

God, why do my brothers go crazy when I have friends over?
> Nicole, age 11

God, what should I do while I wait for You to bring me a best friend at school?
> Lydia, age 9

God, what's it like to be a kitty?
> Hannah, age 9

God, why did You make allergies?
> Zoe, age 10

God, do people have birthdays in heaven?
> Faith, age 11

God, why didn't You let Jesus stay on earth to get married and have children?
> Natalie, age 8

God, what made You want to give Your only Son for so many people?
> Ivy, age 11

God, what is Your favorite color?
> Alyssa, age 10

God, how did You feel when You were on the cross?
> Alexandria, age 10

God, why do people get divorced?
> Faith, age 9

God, where will I be in ten years? What will my life be like?
> Claire, age 10

God, are tomatoes a fruit or a vegetable?
> Abbey, age 10

God, how old are You? Did You just appear? Who is Your mom?
> Eleni, age 9

God, how did You dream up all these humans and their personalities?
> Lisa, age 11

God, how did You make the world?
    Taylor, age 8

God, will I ever get a baby brother or sister?
    Megan, age 9

God, how did You make rainbows?
    Samantha, age 9

God, what does heaven look like?
    Jordanne, age 10

God, why do people smoke?
    Melissa, age 11

God, why did You make lightning?
    Casey, age 8

If you could ask God one question and get an answer right away, what would it be?

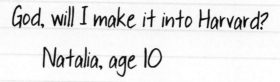

Scan for Video Answers!

God, what does it feel like to rule the world?

Haley, age 9

God, will I make it into Harvard?

Natalia, age 10

God, who will I marry when I grow up?

Gabrielle, age 10

Your Instruction Manual for Living

by Vicki Courtney

Imagine this. It's your birthday, and your family has just gathered in the dining room for a special dinner in your honor. Your mom has fixed your faves—but you can barely eat because you're looking at the pile of presents on the counter. After dinner your dad finally announces it's time for gifts! Excited, you start tearing into them one by one. A new watch! A new shirt! A new backpack! A new . . . what? What is it? Wait! It's your own tablet! Sweet! Your heart beats faster as you take it out of the packaging. You think to yourself, *How will I ever figure this thing out?* Then you see it. Lying perfectly flat at the bottom of the box, almost unnoticed. The instruction manual.

Sometimes I hear people joke about wanting some sort of instruction manual for life. Have you ever felt that way? Do you ever wish someone would tell you how to get through the next few years?

I have good news. God has left us the Bible as our instruction manual. The Bible contains everything you need to know about life—even the upcoming teenage years. Some people say that the Bible is just a book. Nothing special. The Bible is much more than a book like the dictionary or a textbook. The Bible can change lives.

Listen to what one verse says about the Bible: "All Scripture is inspired by God and is profitable for teaching, for rebuking, for correcting, for training in righteousness, so that the man of God may be complete, equipped for every good work" (2 Timothy 3:16–17).

These verses tell us a lot about Scripture. First, God's Word is inspired. This means that God told the people who wrote the Bible exactly what things to write. Remember that tablet? What if it came with two sets of instructions?

If one set was written by a kid and the other set was written by the maker of the tablet, which manual would you trust? Probably the inventor's manual, right? Because God created you and knows you (even the number of hairs on your head!), He knows how to guide you. That instruction is found in the Bible.

Second, the Bible teaches you and me what is true, what is right from wrong. Many people deny the truth of the Bible because they don't want to admit that some of the things they are doing are wrong. If a person can say the Bible is just a book, then that person can just keep living like she wants.

So how do you know the Bible isn't just a random collection of poetry and essays from a bunch of people who lived thousands of years ago? Below are some facts to help you see that the Bible is God's Word—and your guide for living.

ARCHAEOLOGY
(ark-ee-all-oh-gee)

This big word means "the study of really old artifacts." Artifacts are the things that are left over from cities and places buried in the ground hundreds and even thousands of years ago. Have you ever been to a museum and seen dinosaur bones? Those are considered artifacts. The cool thing is that scientists have found artifacts related to people and places in the Bible.

For example, a recent discovery of artifacts shows that the Battle of Jericho really happened the way book of Joshua says it did. Remember how Joshua and his army marched around the city seven times and the walls of the city fell in? Archaeologists digging in that area found evidence that the walls did tumble down just as the Bible said! This is just one example of how archaeology has supported stories in Scripture. In fact, more than 25,000 archeological sites (places where artifacts have been found) have proven that events in the Old Testament occurred the way the Bible said.

Scripture Doesn't Change

Some people think that because the Bible was written in a different language and then put into English, it might not have the same meaning as it did when it was first written. The Bible was originally written in three languages: Hebrew, Greek, and Aramaic. Can you understand those languages? Me neither! Hundreds and hundreds of years ago, people smarter than you and I put the Bible in our language. Here's the cool part: even though the Bible was written long, long ago, the Bible we have today is remarkably similar to the first copies of the Bible. Think about it like this: if you translated the last *Harry Potter* book (over 200,000 words) today and made a bunch of copies from the original book, how accurate do you think the copies would be in 1,500 years? There's one difference between then and now—the copies back then were handwritten! Even though individual scribes copied the Scripture, the meaning of the words has not changed. The vast majority of the differences in the copies are nothing more than spelling or grammar errors. Those are the kinds of things that don't change the meaning of the Bible—God loves you, Jesus died for you, and you can have eternal life.

You can't ask for a more trustworthy instruction manual than the Bible. Trust me; this is one book worth reading . . . and rereading and rereading.

All Scripture is inspired by God and is profitable for teaching, for rebuking, for correcting, for training in righteousness, so that the man of God may be complete, equipped for every good work.
—2 Timothy 3:16–17

How to Become a Christian

by Vicki Courtney

Becoming a Christian is the most important decision you will ever make in your life. Read each step below very carefully to make sure understand what each one means.

We learn about God's love in the Bible.

"For God so loved the world that he gave his one and only Son, that whoever believes in him shall not perish but have eternal life."—John 3:16 NIV

Perish means to die and to be apart from God—forever. God loves you so much and wants you to have *eternal life* in heaven where you are with him forever.

If you understand what John 3:16 means, put a check here: _____

All of us have sinned.

For all have sinned and fall short of the glory of God.—Romans 3:23

You may have heard someone say, "I'm only human—nobody's perfect." This Bible verse says the same thing: We are all sinners. No one is perfect. We do things that are wrong, things that fall short of "God's glorious standard."

Imagine that God gives you a test. You would have to make a 100 to meet God's standard because God is perfect. Because God is perfect and we are not, it is impossible for anyone to make a 100 on this test! Before you start to worry that you don't meet His standard (you won't make a 100), just wait—there's good news ahead.

If you understand what Romans 3:23 means, put a check here: _____

Sin has a penalty (punishment).

For the wages [cost] of sin is death.—Romans 6:23 (NIV)

Our punishment is separation from God's blessings, favor, and love. When we die, we will receive God's wrath for all eternity unless payment is made for sin. The Bible teaches that those who choose to reject God will spend eternity in a place called hell. You may have heard some bad things about hell, but the worst part about hell is that you are separated from God forever.

If you understand what Romans 6:23 means, put a check here: _____

Christ has paid the price for our sins!

But God proves His own love for us in that while we were still sinners, Christ died for us. —Romans 5:8

The Bible teaches that Jesus Christ is the perfect Son of God. He never sinned, and He has paid the price for all your sins. The Bible says that Christ loved you enough to die for you. Pretty amazing!

If you understand what Romans 5:8 means, put a check here: _____

Salvation (being saved from the penalty of your sins) is a free gift.

For you are saved by grace through faith, and this is not from yourselves; it is God's gift—not from works, so that no one can boast.—Ephesians 2:8–9

The word grace means "a gift we don't deserve." That gift is forgiveness from your sins and eternal life. God's gift to you is free. You do not have to work for a gift. That's why it's called a gift. All you have to do is receive it. Believe with all your heart that Jesus Christ died for you and paid the price for your sins!

If you understand what Ephesians 2:8–9 means, put a check here: _____

You must receive Him.

But to all who did receive Him, He gave them the right to be children of God.—John 1:12

Christ has died for your sins so you can be forgiven. However, you must choose to believe in Him and give Him control of your life. When you receive Christ into your heart, you become a child of God. The Christian life is a personal relationship (just like you have with a best friend) with God through Jesus Christ. He never takes His gift back, so you don't have to worry about losing it. It is yours forever.

If you understand what John 1:12 means, put a check here: _____

So, what do you think about God's offer of forgiveness? Is this a gift you want to accept? If so, tell God. You don't have to say a fancy prayer—just talk to Him and tell Him that you believe that Jesus died on the cross for your sins and you want Him to save you. That's all it takes! Stop and say a prayer right now.

Did you say a prayer and accept God's gift of forgiveness? _____

If you answered "yes," congratulations! You are a Christian! If you aren't quite sure you are ready to accept God's gift of forgiveness, talk to someone who can help—your pastor, parents, or a relative. Tell them you want to know more about being a Christian!

(Adapted from "Your Christian Life," Billy Graham Evangelistic Association, 1997)

Last Word on God:

"I am the Alpha and the Omega," says the Lord God, "the One who is, who was, and who is coming, the Almighty."
—Revelation 1:8

Can You Relate?

1. Have you ever wondered if the things the Bible says about Jesus are true? Do you believe Jesus is the Son of God and came to save us from the penalty of our sins?

2. Proverbs 1:10 says, "My son, if sinners entice you, don't be persuaded." Can you think of a time when you were tempted by sin? What are some temptations that entice girls your age?

3. To "fear the Lord" is to show Him respect. Share examples of how tweens show disrespect toward God. Then share examples of how you can show respect for God.

4. Have you ever prayed using the ACTS model of prayer? What does ACTS stand for? Write down a prayer below using the ACTS model.

5. Did you come with an instruction manual? If so, what is it?

6. The Bible says, "All Scripture is inspired by God and is profitable for teaching, for rebuking, for correcting, for training in righteousness, so that the man of God may be complete, equipped for every good work" (2 Timothy 3:16–17). Put this in your own words.

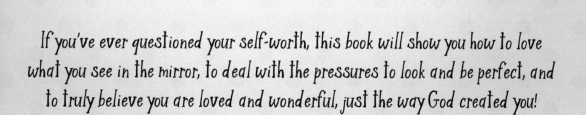

Don't miss Vicki Courtney's
next book for tween girls:

What About Me?

Seeing Yourself the Way God Sees You

If you've ever questioned your self-worth, this book will show you how to love what you see in the mirror, to deal with the pressures to look and be perfect, and to truly believe you are loved and wonderful, just the way God created you!

Available September 2016